Crisis
Communications

WITHDRAWN

# Crisis
# Communications
## in the 24/7 Social Media World

## A Guidebook for CEOs and Public Relations Professionals

## Bill Walker

Paramount Market Publishing, Inc.

Paramount Market Publishing, Inc.
950 Danby Road, Suite 136
Ithaca, NY 14850
www.paramountbooks.com
Phone: 607-275-8100; 888-787-8100
Fax: 607-275-8101

Publisher: James Madden
Editorial Director: Doris Walsh

This publication is designed to provide accurate and authoritative information in regard to the subject matter covered. It is sold with the understanding that the publisher is not engaged in rendering legal, accounting, or other professional services. If legal advice or other expert assistance is required, the services of a competent professional should be sought.

All trademarks are the property of their respective companies.

Cataloging in Publication Data available
ISBN-10: 1-941688-22-5 | ISBN-13: 978-1-941688-22-9

*For Iris*

# Contents

# Chapter 1

# Lightning Strikes

DOWN DEEP, you know a crisis will strike you or your organization. You're just not sure when it will happen, or what it will be.

And in most cases, you're not sure exactly how it actually will be handled.

But that's a "tomorrow problem."

It shouldn't be.

You cannot afford it to be.

Today's crisis communications environment is more explosive and more potentially devastating to both your brand and your own career than ever before.

In today's hyper-connected world, information travels at the speed of a mouse click and opinions are formed in the time it takes to read 140 characters or glance at a picture.

The single undeniable truth about the otherwise complex business of crisis communications is that it's all about the collision between your instincts and the public's expectations.

Things are happening to you so quickly in the high-speed internet world of a crisis that you don't have much choice initially, other than to react on instinct. The problem is, the public's rush-to-judgment is equally rapid. Often your first reaction—your instinct—is the only one you'll be judged on, positively or negatively.

Those are very high stakes.

Unless you stack the deck in your favor.

That's what this book is all about.

Walk away, right now, if you're expecting a step-by-step "how to" of crisis communications. Look elsewhere if you are hoping to see lists such as *The 17 Commandments of Crisis Communications* or *The 5 Things You Need to do Now to Prepare for a Crisis*. These lists are always filled with words like "Identify" and "Control" and "Respond" and "Assess" and "Anticipate." They are fine and pithy and so forth, but I have never seen anyone actually use a list like that during a crisis.

Imagine in the heat of the moment someone stops your senior management team meeting in the early hours of a crisis by saying: "Hold on! Have we *Identified* as per No. 3 on our list?" It just doesn't happen, much less have any material impact on the outcome of the crisis itself and what is left of your company or organization's reputation.

I have worked in daily media (newspapers) and PR for more than three decades now and I am more convinced than ever that the single biggest factor determining the success or failure of a person, organization, or company when a crisis suddenly strikes is their gut reaction.

It influences your approach in ways you don't even realize in the heat of the moment.

Now, with this book in your hands, you have a choice: you can gamble that life experience will lead to you make good decisions instinctively, or you can join me on a journey to explore the realities of what your reaction is likely to be, what it should be, and the approach you can take to produce a winning outcome for your organization's reputation.

It's about reducing the risk and significantly increasing your odds of success.

Because as John F. Kennedy once famously said, "The word 'crisis' when written in Chinese, is composed of two characters. One represents danger and the other represents opportunity."

Others in politics are fond of saying "Never let a good crisis go to waste." There is truth in these statements. A crisis need not be something your organization fears. You can embrace it as an opportunity to help define what your company stands for, to build brand loyalty, engage your employees and stakeholders, and to break through to the next level. As a CEO or senior leader, you can use it to define your own leadership style, beliefs, and standards.

The objective is to help you avoid some of the most common mistakes people make when confronted by a crisis.

These mistakes are often what would be described as honest in the sense that there was no evil intent. Most are instinctive reactions. There is no silver bullet, no PR strategy, no PR advisor senior and skilled enough, to help people whose instinct is to lie. In fact, there is nothing in the entire world of PR that can save someone from the lie. The best we can hope for is that we can convince that person to approach the situation differently and not to lie in the first place.

We have a saying in journalism: The truth will always "out" eventually. It's not grammatically correct but reporters use a lot of short forms in language when they're not writing.

Cyclist Lance Armstrong is a classic example. Betsy Andreu, the wife of Armstrong's former teammate Frankie Andreu, spent a decade relentlessly trying to convince members of the media that Armstrong was doping. Behind the scenes, according to reports mentioned in *Sports Illustrated,* Armstrong's people whispered (not for attribution) that she was vindictive and just plain crazy. Reporters ignored her calls and emails. But this Michigan-based mom who spent her time ferrying her three kids to Little League and hockey games, was anything but crazy.

She held a laser-like determination that the truth about Armstrong and the lie that was his brand would be revealed. *Sports Illustrated* called her the Erin Brockovich of the cycling world. When Armstrong finally admitted to Oprah Winfrey what he did, Andreu was vindicated (her story is wonderfully told in the documentary *The Armstrong Lie*) and the principle that the truth will always out was proven again. If you've ever witnessed someone prosper by covering something up, or lying, don't fret. Just wait. That day of reckoning will come.

Given the lightening speed crises travel in this era of social media, the need to react correctly has never been more imperative. And there has never been less forgiveness for those who react improperly in that first moment of the crisis spotlight, even if they only reacted on instinct. There is very little margin for error.

Your first reaction, what you tell the public and your stakeholders right off the bat, will be widely disseminated at the speed of sound. There is no going back from there, any more than it's possible to get the toothpaste back in the tube. Your first utterances, if a mistake, will form part of the gotcha narrative in a popular, ratings-enhancing feeding frenzy to take you and your company down and fast.

This reality was my No. 1 motivation for writing this book, to give leaders like you a sense of perspective about how you will feel when a crisis descends upon you, how you'll instinctively react, and how you can be very deliberate about taking a counter-intuitive approach in order to be successful at crisis communications.

What we're talking about is fighting your initial instincts. You will recognize them for what they are. You can speak to your employees and leadership team about how they will be feeling when a crisis strikes, so that they too can understand the tendencies we all share.

But most importantly, you can really begin to understand public expectations. There are things you can learn about your company and your organization, about the sector you work in, even about yourself, that will guide you before the crisis hits.

We will explore the rush-to-judgment phenomenon so prevalent today and what that means to you. It's also critical that you understand the court of public opinion and the rules of evidence that may apply in law versus the rules that will apply to you during your crisis.

Ultimately it is about that knife's edge you will be on at a time of crisis.

You can react predictably and reinforce every negative perception the public already holds. That will result in a very rapid, very painful outcome.

Or you can understand this environment and be smarter about how you react. You can shatter those expectations. You can win.

# Chapter 2

# The Court of Public Opinion

IMAGINE that you are accused of a crime, and before you even have the opportunity to hire a lawyer, much less consider whether to plead guilty or not guilty, you are marched to court. You walk in the door of the courtroom. They have been waiting for you. Someone immediately looks at you and stands up. "Guilty as charged!" A jury of your peers has already rendered its verdict. Your head is spinning.

Except that instead of a jury of 12 peers, the jury is made up of millions on social media, plus your customers, shareholders, stakeholders, government officials, even your own employees. Fairness? Due process? A level playing field? Put all of those notions out of your mind—completely. That is not the way crisis communications environments exist. And that is why it is so difficult to operate in this environment, and why many of us find it so fascinating.

When you are managing a crisis, or preparing your team for one, you need to set aside all expectations related to fairness. The best psychological place to get to is: "I am guilty until proven innocent." Thanks, in part, to 4G mobile phone speeds and DSL cable internet connections, we live in a world of not just instant gratification, but instant judgment. Get comfortable with the fact that 140 characters is not just the limit of a tweet, it is very close to the limit of information most people feel they need before making a judgment about you.

I don't mean that as a criticism of the public, or of the rush-to-judgment phenomenon we live with in today's modern media. It is just a reality of the online pace at which we now live our lives. President Obama told the White House press corps after the Boston Marathon bombing, "In this age of reporting and instant Tweets and blogs, there is a temptation to latch on to any information and sometimes to jump to conclusions. But when a tragedy like this happens . . . we (need to) take care not to rush to judgment."

Harvard grad David Friedman, a legal expert, economist and physicist, was moved to write a blog post called *The Rush to Judgment*[1] that revolved around the Facebook-driven national media story about a New Jersey waitress and ex-Marine who said a couple refused to give her a tip and instead scribbled on their bill that they refused to do so because they disagreed with her gay lifestyle. Thousands on Facebook and millions of TV viewers and other consumers of media condemned the purportedly bigoted behavior of the unnamed couple. Hundreds of sympathetic people sent the waitress money, to cover the tip. Yet the story turned out to be a hoax. The couple in question came forward[2] with a time-stamped copy of their bill which proved they paid an $18 tip on a $93 check—a 20 percent tip. The family also told a New York TV news program that the handwriting on the bill didn't match their own handwriting.

By now the story of a homophobic slur that was a hoax had become an international news sensation. But to Friedman, the behavior of the waitress was less interesting than the behavior of the thousands on Facebook and in the media who rushed to judgment and immediately believed her story without checking any of the facts. Eventually all the facts came out. The waitress in question was described by former co-workers as a serial liar who had once shaved her head and claimed to have brain cancer; who had dramatically overstated the extent of damage to her home caused by Hurricane Sandy; and who Pentagon officials went to the trouble to admit to journalists had been dishonorably discharged.[3]

## Where Expectations Come From

The case Freidman cites is a reflection of what I consider the general public's conditioning which, in large part, sets the crisis environment. It's a conditioning caused by people making a connection with outcomes they have seen or heard before, whether those outcomes are real or just urban myths. You've seen them all in one form or another: big corporation tramples little consumer; travel company rips off family who saved all year for their vacation; large manufacturer found to be secretly dumping chemicals in the river; the broker with his hand in the cookie jar of money his clients trusted him to invest; or perhaps the most common of all, the scandal-plagued politician fighting for his or her own survival. We make these judgments not just in terms of the scandals we see in the news. We do it in our everyday lives. For example, many studies have shown that one of the most common mistakes managers make in the workplace is a rush-to-judgment based on preconceived notions[4] about employee behavior, rather than looking at each employee as unique, a blank slate.

> One of the most common mistakes managers make in the workplace is a rush-to-judgment based on preconceived notions about employee behavior.

I believe you can trace public opinion conditioning back to long before the internet era, to the 1972–74 Nixon White House Watergate scandal and the so-called "Watergate effect." It's not that public cynicism didn't exist prior to Watergate, initially dismissed by Nixon's press secretary as "a third-rate burglary attempt."[5] But numerous academics have written about the sea change in public attitudes towards politics, politicians, and institutions that followed the greatest scandal in American history and the only presidential resignation ever. It spawned generations of investigative journalists who uncovered more scandals and crises, which further entrenched that cynicism—in most cases rightly so. The impact continues today. When the media seizes on what it considers a major controversy, they tend to name it with the appendage "-gate"; for example: "Bridgegate," New Jersey Governor Chris Christie's staff allegedly punishing a political rival by causing massive traffic jams;

"Hackgate" (also known as "Rupertgate" or "Murdochgate"), the former *News of the World* scandal involving the alleged hacking of cell phones; "Memogate" (a.k.a. "Rathergate"), a forged memo about President George W. Bush's military record that led to the resignation of Dan Rather as anchor of the *CBS Evening News;* and there have been countless others.

The reality of public opinion today is that people are bombarded with more news than ever before, and much of it bad news. In the 1970s and 1980s you needed to catch the 6 or 11 P.M. news or read the newspaper that landed on your doorstep, or catch the radio news at the top of the hour in your car, to hear about what was going on. Today we are connected 24/7. News channels are broadcasting around the clock, in every language and in every country. Main network channels break in to scheduled programs routinely to deliver breaking news. Think about the volumes we see during the Olympic Games. At the 2014 Sochi Games, NBC aired 1,539 hours of coverage on its networks, including NBC, NBC Sports Network, the USA Network, and CNBC, plus it added another 1,000 hours of live coverage online at NBCOlympics. com and fed coverage into two NBC tablet apps. That is more coverage than the Vancouver and Torino Olympics combined.[6]

When Alvin Toffler wrote about information overload in his 1970 book *Future Shock,* he was referring to the inability of people to make decisions because they were bombarded with too much information. I believe he accurately predicted where we find ourselves today. Some have calculated that, in terms of information that comes at each of us daily, we receive the equivalent of 174 newspapers worth of information a day, 365 days a year (based on an average 85-page newspaper).[7] Another study showed the average person processed the equivalent of 100,500 words per day worth of information.[8] Compare that number to the number of times we blink our eyes every day, about 28,000 times.[9] There is so much information that people have coined the phrase "infobesity" to describe this overload, arguing that infobesity can lead to a lack of productivity and bad decision making.[10] As a result, some experts now say that people need to go on information "diets" designed to cut out so-called "junk information" and clear their minds to allow themselves to be more productive and alert.[11] People who suffer from infobesity cannot, for example, stop texting their friends while they drive their cars. Various jurisdictions across North America have increased fines and other penalties for texting and driving, but the problem persists—because, as infobesity experts will tell you, people are addicted to information overload in this digital era we live in.

> People are addicted to information overload in this digital era we live in.

What that means is that people have very little time or capacity (or patience) to consider the facts before they judge you or your organization during a crisis. With the information overload people are suffering, the easiest thing to do is to attach the scenario they are hearing to a memory of something they heard or learned about before, essentially categorizing it. It's much simpler to categorize something than to figure out a new meaning or significance. That's what the so-called Citizen Journalists do when they start to talk about your crisis on Twitter or Facebook. Those social media conversations are then picked up by the mainstream media. Every single day there is a crisis, or an alleged scandal, somewhere—in fact dozens and dozens of them—far too many for members of the public to explore in a factual way. It's easier to get a drive-by picture and move on; after all, we still have the equivalent of 173 more newspapers to take in that day.

## Public Conditioning

And so in a Pavlovian way, the public's responses are conditioned by the simplistic reactions that tend to predominate. If they see a tweet about a cruise line company doing something untoward with its passengers, they are conditioned by many recent events in the media and in social media to assume the worst. If it is a Facebook post about auto insurance, people have a conditioned response that somehow, the insurance company will find a technical loophole to deny coverage. A politician using public influence for private gain? Conditioned response. Ask yourself: How many times have you heard someone say, "Well, we all know that all politicians are crooked anyway." Or someone trying to get through on the phone for help from a bureaucrat in a government office who finally turns around in frustration and says, "They don't give a damn about us, those lazy government employees." Need to call a 1-800 number to address a billing problem with a cable company or cell phone provider? Nightmare. People expect the worst and are surprised when it doesn't happen. We'll get to that later. These preconceived notions even apply to mainstream journalism: Politicians across North America now commonly run against the media, tapping into the public's predisposition to believe that journalists either don't tell the truth or they tell such a biased version of events that they are not to be believed or trusted.

That is why when your crisis hits, people are likely to look up from their lives, see it, and say, "Yes, here we go again." You need to be ready for that reaction. And keep in mind that you are too close to it; you have both an emotional and intellectual connection to your company or organization that the public simply doesn't share.

> When your crisis hits, people are likely to look up from their lives, see it, and say, "Here we go again."

The truth is, the reason so many companies or organizations fail in crisis communications scenarios is that they fail to understand this environment. They don't understand the rules of the game. They cannot seem to grasp the concept. They believe people will understand what they go through every day and how hard they have worked in the past to ensure the crisis would not occur. These business or organization leaders say to each other, "Surely they will give us some credit and cut us some slack here."

No. Absolutely not. People do not care. They don't care because they just don't know what you've done in the past. They don't know because you probably haven't told them. But even if you have, either they weren't listening, or they heard you and they still don't care. "It's happening now! This is affecting me, and my family, now! So what are you going to do about it? Stop trying to cheat me! Stop trying to cover this up and make it go away!" That is the rush-to-judgment. That's what you need to be prepared for. It's the environment you will be stepping into.

So why should you venture into that environment, if it is so negative? Perhaps you are thinking, why should you engage at all if the deck is firmly stacked against you in a crisis? "They're going to crucify us anyway, so let's just hunker down and ride out the storm. It will blow over." It's a fair question.

In fact, in criminal law circles, many lawyers believe defendants make terrible witnesses. Whether they truly are bad witnesses in terms of not being credible, or not communicating clearly, is beside the point. The real reason lawyers believe this is that in a court of law the onus is on the prosecution to prove guilt. Why help the prosecution by opening up the defendant to cross-examination? The defendant is innocent until proven guilty. If the defendant doesn't testify, he or she cannot be cross-examined by the prosecutor. As I hope we've established here, the opposite is true in the court of public opinion. You are guilty until proven innocent. You can't decline to testify on your own behalf. Even if you could, it wouldn't prevent you from being cross-examined, because the public is the prosecutor. They are already cross-examining you and, in all likelihood, convicting you for being guilty as charged.

> In the court of public opinion you are guilty until proven innocent.

## A Classic Example

BP's 2010 Deepwater Horizon oil spill in the Gulf of Mexico is a classic modern-day example of this. When former CEO Anthony Hayward initially referred to the spill's impact as "very, very modest" and "relatively tiny" the comments were viewed as disastrous from a public relations standpoint. It was like waving a red cape at the proverbial bull of public opinion. People registered cover-up just as they have countless times since Watergate. Many people associated what they were hearing with the *Exxon Valdez* oil spill. They instinctively understood it was Hayward's job to minimize the damage to the company by minimizing how he characterized the spill. However, his comments had the opposite effect—they actually led to people believing the damage in the Gulf would be much more widespread and devastating, a view the media seized upon. Hayward's words came back to haunt him when this, in fact, turned out to be true. That further entrenched the public's conditioned response about so-called "rich oil executives" and in that sense, set the entire resource industry back in terms of reputation.

The crisis was destined for every crisis communications "worst ever" list the day Hayward famously looked into a TV camera, clearly frustrated, and said, "I'd like my life back." His statement was contrasted against seagulls and fish—coated in black, sticky oil—laying on blackened beaches. Gulf residents said it was likely that their lives would never get back to normal. The families of eleven men who died on the BP rig when it exploded also knew they would not get their lives back. This was a fatal blow and soon, Hayward was out as CEO. I would argue Hayward was finished the moment he said the words—the rest was just about arranging the timing and financial terms. The odd thing was that Hayward was, and is, a highly respected veteran of his industry. It could be that he self-selected the exit ramp by saying what he did, consciously or unconsciously. Meanwhile, to this day, BP is still trying to make things right in the Gulf.

It is my view that Hayward, and BP, never really understood the crisis environment in 2010. Which is just extraordinary, when you think about it. I have no doubt that they were conducting extensive public opinion polling. But they were also likely riveted by their then-plummeting stock price and their seeming inability to do anything about it.

The public was conditioned to believe that BP would not tell the whole story and be completely truthful. Every time BP said something that turned out to be untrue or obscured reality, it was a check mark in the public's cynicism column. When Hayward called the spill "relatively tiny" and it turned out to be a massive catastrophe, the largest oil spill in the history of the petroleum industry globally—check. When BP promised several short-term fixes (most notably it's "top kill" strategy) and they all failed—check. When people learned Hayward had sold one-third of his shares in BP about a month before the accident—although no one has ever proven he had prior knowledge of the impending tragedy—for many it was—"check." When he attended a ritzy yacht race while seagulls, coated in black oil, staggered around on the sandy Gulf beaches—check.

That is why this is the first topic I am tackling, after the introduction. If there is nothing else you, as a reader, take away from this book, my wish would be that it is this lesson:

**You need to accept the crisis environment you will be entering.**

Understand it now. To be miles ahead of where you would otherwise be and avoid time-wasting actions and negative, unproductive reactions, you need to accept the upside-down rules of the court of public opinion in crisis communications. You have to understand that now is not the time to cover up, but to open up. You must be determined, from the very first minute, to focus on the public interest, not your self-interest. And most importantly, you need to set out to shatter public expectations of what you will do next, not reinforce negative stereotypes and the public's preconceived notions about you.

That has to be the foundation upon which all of your crisis preparations and policies are constructed. Otherwise, you are doomed to failure before you have even begun to react. At the very least, failing to grasp the reality of today's crisis communications environment will stack the odds heavily against you.

Here's the bottom line: People think you are guilty. The public's first thought is that you are probably still hiding something. The public's second thought is not surprise, but recognition (of a past negative perception). The media won't be satisfied with your answers. Stakeholders will demand answers. Your employees will feel alienated and out of the loop. They will be more concerned with their own futures than the future of the company. You will be flamed on social media.

(Oh, and your cell phone battery will die at the worst possible moment.)

Those are the realities.

Accept these realities now and you will already be miles ahead of where most people are, both strategically and psychologically, when the crisis hits.

## Notes

1. http://daviddfriedman.blogspot.ca/2013/11/the-rush-to-judgement.html
2. www.usatoday.com/story/news/nation/2013/11/26/waitress-no-tip-hoax/3761565/
3. www.huffingtonpost.com/2013/12/05/dayna-morales-suspended_n_4391753.html
4. https://www.washington.edu/facilities/orgrel/files/documents/leadership/052012_management_mistakes.pdf
5. http://articles.philly.com/1997-06-15/news/25526526_1_scandal-in-american-history-watergate-president-richard-nixon
6. www.forbes.com/sites/dorothypomerantz/2014/02/04/get-ready-for-more-olympics-coverage-and-more-ads-than-ever-before/
7. www.telegraph.co.uk/science/science-news/8316534/Welcome-to-the-information-age-174-newspapers-a-day.html
8. http://hmi.ucsd.edu/howmuchinfo_research_report_consum.php
9. www.huffingtonpost.com/2012/12/30/why-do-we-blink-so-much-mental-rest_n_2377720.html
10. www.infobesity.com/node/1
11. www.informationdiet.com/

# Chapter 3

# Fight or Flight Response

MOST OF US have had that heart-in-your-throat experience of a near car accident. You are driving along, relaxed. Maybe you are thinking about plans for the weekend ahead. Or listening to a song and reflecting on the memories it brings back. When suddenly—panic! A vehicle appears out of nowhere. You see it in your peripheral vision. It is headed right at you. You slam on the brakes. Grip the steering wheel tighter. Your body surges with adrenaline. Afterward, crash averted, your heart pounds. Your whole body feels like it is slightly vibrating. You feel 100 times more awake than you were just a split second ago. But you know your body needs to slow down, and gradually it does start to return to normal. You can feel the stress slowly drain away.

The *fight or flight* response your body experiences in this situation is very real. The term was coined in 1932 by Harvard physiologist Walter Bradford Cannon (1871–1945). He came up with the phrase based on his experimental observations of animals' physiological reactions to pain, fear, and rage. Cannon found the same in humans and coined another term, *homeostasis*, which essentially refers to the human body's ability to self-regulate in different conditions.[1]

In fight or flight—similar to the near-miss car accident—it is amazing what the human brain instantaneously does for us. It dilates our pupils so we can take in the maximum amount of light. It tenses our muscles to prepare us for maximum physical exertion. It even shuts down our non-essential systems like digestion so that the body can focus the maximum amount of energy possible on the threat at hand. Breathing becomes more rapid and heart rate increases because both help power the system; meanwhile adrenaline is released into the system for that extra turbo boost.

But the truth is, most of the time our fight or flight response is triggered it turns out to be a false alarm, such as the near-miss car accident. That is because the system in the brain that triggers the response is automatic and cannot distinguish between a real threat and a perceived threat that is no danger at all.[2] Still, the automated way the system responds is critically important here. Cannon found that in nature, the system is what told a zebra, for example, to run (flight) from a lion; while the lion would have had the same physiological reaction that led to his attack (fight). In humans, we would never want a system that, after many false alarms, decided the next fear trigger was the boy who cried wolf, and therefore didn't automatically activate. Better safe than sorry. That is why our bodies tense up automatically when we slip on a set of stairs and begin to fall; it is our muscles and reflexes trying to protect us. That is also why we flinch when someone pretends to throw a punch at us—it is a perceived danger that our body automatically adjusts for by turning our head away—as opposed to sticking our chin out.

You will have that initial tendency to flinch—which in some cases can be a huge and costly mistake.

What you need to be crystal clear about in terms of crisis communications is that you will have that initial tendency to flinch—which in some cases can be a huge and costly mistake. You will have a tendency to automatically go into self-protection mode.

Whole Foods CEO John Mackey said that's exactly how he felt when the FCC investigated him for posting on the Yahoo Financial online bulletin board under a screen-name pseudonym about an impending Whole Foods takeover target. The story was leaked to the *Wall Street Journal* and suddenly it was "a huge scandal" he told *Inc.* magazine's on-stage *Inc. Live* series of talks. Mackey was accused of all sorts of misdeeds, including trying to suppress the stock price of his takeover target. Soon both the SEC and the Whole Foods board of directors had launched investigations. He said the board instructed him not to defend himself, blog, or speak to the media, ". . . so there was this field day of smearing me. It was very, very, very painful." He said this went on for day after day. "I think the natural human response in that situation is to basically contract. To go back someplace or find someplace that is really safe. Where it doesn't hurt so much. What I found is a better strategy is to basically do the opposite. Instead of contracting into fear, expand and open up more." And for him, Mackey said, that meant learning an entirely new skill set.

## The Tendency to Deny

Depending on how serious or catastrophic the crisis is, your body might actually experience a version of the flight or flight response, for example if the crisis has led to deaths as has been the case in several events involving Listeriosis contamination in food. But for the most part, I am talking now about a response that, while similar, is not physiological. It is more psychological. It is our natural tendency to defend. It is a natural tendency to choose the crisis communications version of the flight option. Very seldom in crisis communications cases have I seen companies or CEOs actually counter-attack; the equivalent of the fight response is seldom triggered initially. It sometimes happens later when someone decides to sue, or an organization becomes angry because of the perception of being treated unfairly.

Think about it this way: You are attending a Major League Baseball game on a beautiful summer day, hot dog in hand. Life doesn't get much better. Then, in a split second after hearing the crack of the bat everyone around you jumps and out of the corner of your eye you see that foul ball headed straight at you. Your instinct is to duck, to cover up. Now your T-shirt is covered in mustard. Even people sitting directly behind home plate can be seen on television flinching during the first few innings when a pitch is fouled right back into the screen. They flinch even though when they took their seats they knew they were protected from this danger by the screen. It's pure instinct.

Understanding our instinctive tendency in a crisis situation is almost as important as what we discussed in Chapter 2 about the crisis communications environment and the court of public opinion. That's because the public's conditioning that we talked about includes conditioning to believe that you or your company or organization will act, out of instinct, to protect yourself and not them—not the consumer or customer. They are conditioned to believe you will act in your own self-interest, not the public interest.

That is why it didn't surprise people to hear the BP CEO initially call the Gulf oil spill "relatively tiny." It was consistent with what they believed an oil executive would do, namely downplay the spill and try to maintain operations and maximize profit for shareholders regardless of the impact on the environment. Even if the company's intentions toward the environment were good, most would still expect company spokespersons to defend their people and defend their actions. Not to say it is necessarily wrong to defend—the point is that this is what the public has been conditioned to expect.

And that is what makes the difference between people who are extraordinarily successful at crisis communications and issues management; and those who repeatedly fail. It is the difference between CEOs, companies or organizations that respond in a way that truly surprises the public because it goes against their conditioned expectations; and organizations that respond in ways that simply reinforce the conditioned negative expectations the public have.

Two startling and opposite Canadian examples were apparent on Boxing Day, 2013. In one case, a major furniture chain called The Brick advised its followers on Facebook that although online buyers were told they would get an additional 50 percent discount when they took their online shopping cart to check out, that was a mistake, due to a "computer glitch," and the company would not honor the discount.[3] At the exact same time, Delta announced that it would, in fact, honor the vastly reduced prices[4] of flights that were the result of an online glitch, including for example, a flight from New York City to Los Angeles for $47.

The Brick confirmed the conditioned expectation of the public, namely that a discount furniture retailer would hook people in with a "too good to be true" offer and then rescind it. Delta, on the other hand, defied expectations. By honoring the mistaken discount, Delta went against the conditioned expectations of many travelers that airline companies will try to pry every nickel and dime they possibly can from your wallet, including bag fees, food fees, seat fees, etc.

As a result, Delta earned widespread praise on Twitter and Facebook, likely influencing millions of people positively toward its brand. The Brick, on the other hand, was torched on social media with many people saying they would never shop at the store again. Many more likely formed a negative view of the furniture store brand based on what they saw from friends and family on social media. To extend the fight or flight analogy, The Brick instinctively protected its own interests, not the public or consumer interest. Delta, on the other hand, acted in the consumer's interest and took the short-term financial hit. Delta is the clear winner here in terms of longer-term reputation management and customer loyalty.

## A Different Response

I must share with you another great example of winning by defying public conditioning—of shattering expectations. Chip Kelly, head coach of the Philadelphia Eagles, paved his path to the NFL through his coaching successes at the University of Oregon. In Fall 2009, Kelly's Oregon team was considered a contender for the national championship. And that's why fan Tony Seminary traveled to neighboring Idaho to watch his beloved Oregon Ducks open the season against Boise State.

Embarrassingly, Oregon lost the game with a lackluster effort, and to make matters worse, their star running back got frustrated and punched a Boise State player in the face. Now, this couldn't be classified as a crisis situation unless you happened to be the most die-hard Ducks fan. Certainly to Seminary it was. And he wanted to do something about it.

So he did something unusual. He emailed Kelly an invoice for $439, the travel costs related to attending the game, with a note that said: "The product on the field Thursday night is not something I was at all proud of, and I feel as though I'm entitled to my money back for the trip."[5] Seminary thought that would be the end of it, point made. But he received an emailed reply from Kelly: "What is your address?" Soon, an envelope showed up in Seminary's mailbox containing a check for $439, signed by Kelly. It was a classic case of surprising a customer with a gesture that went against everything the customer was conditioned to believe. Did it win Kelly any brand loyalty from this customer? Did it help insulate Kelly from potential future slip-ups in this customer's mind? "I think of coach Kelly as a totally different person now," Seminary told the college football website *everydayshouldbesaturday.com*. "Let's just say he lost every game as Oregon coach. You would never hear me calling for his head. It just wouldn't happen. The guy showed an incredible amount of class."

## Lead with Your Chin

Think of it as leading with your chin. Very few people, when they see a punch coming toward their face, will actually jut their chin out. Let's face it, very few people would have paid that fan's invoice, as Kelly did. Most throw up their hands protectively and duck away, or "contract" to a safer place, as Whole Foods CEO Mackey said. This is where crisis communications is most counter-intuitive. Yes, the court of public opinion is the opposite of what we would normally expect in a court of law, but we can compensate for that by communicating proactively and keeping our promises to ensure our audiences are kept up to date (more on that later). But it is very difficult to overcome an organization's collective reflex toward self-defense. And this can be fatal to your crisis communications outcome, particularly given the lightning speed at which these situations play out.

Given how quickly you need to react, the chances are greater that there will be something instinctive about how you react; and that the discussions around the boardroom table with your CEO and executive team will have an initial reactive tone; a defensive tone. Initially, nobody wants to believe a crisis can turn out to be as bad as it often turns out to be. Better safe than sorry? Imagine if the human body's Fight or Flight response didn't kick in that one time when we actually needed it. Disaster. So the tendency toward initial defensiveness needs to be recognized and accounted for.

Surprisingly it's still far too common a mistake to be defensive in the early hours of a crisis (see the BP example). Given ample and repeated evidence of how badly things turn out for organizations that react in ways that confirm the public's conditioned negative expectations, it's mind-boggling to see so many companies and organizations do exactly that. What's worse is the fact that your organization's initial reaction to the crisis will set a "storyline" on social media and in the mainstream media that is nearly impossible to change as the issue develops. Quite the opposite actually. It's like it is set in stone.

On social media and in mainstream media, there will be a desire to further amplify that original storyline as the crisis goes on. So, if you are defensive and perceived to be acting in your own self-interest at first, the attitudes formed are extremely unlikely to change later, no matter how you try to set things right. People will always repeat the fact that your initial reaction was a defensive one. You will "fit" into that category the public has been so heavily pre-conditioned to expect you to fit into. It's only if you shatter that pre-conditioned expectation that the public will look at you more objectively, and will tend

> If you are perceived to be acting in your own self-interest at first, the attitudes formed are extremely unlikely to change later.

to view you as something different or something smarter or more caring. As we will get into in the chapters ahead, you will need to focus not on how your bosses, board members, or shareholders view the situation in the short-term, but what is right for the long-term health of your organization. This is clearly easier to accomplish with privately held corporations than with publicly traded ones, but the same rules apply.

## The Three Strikes

This is where you need to think about the three strikes rule. In crisis communications it works like baseball, with a significant twist. In baseball every strike is equal. A two-strike home run is just as good as a home run with zero strikes against. That is just not the case in crisis communications. In this situation each strike against is twice as damaging to your organization's reputation as the strike before it. The negative impact multiplies.

The first strike, which is usually the initial instinctive defensive response (feeding the public's preconceived notions), means that the next time something inevitably goes wrong during your crisis (strike two), even through no fault of your own, it will be twice as damaging to your brand. The two acts by your organization will be tied together into one negative overall impression. Then, even if the third strike is another development essentially outside of your control, it can often be the near-fatal blow to the brand. It's safe to say the third time isn't the charm. So think about this: If the very first, defensive, strike had been avoided and instead good will had been created by a consumer-friendly, public-interest response, that brand equity is more likely to prompt the public to see the second strike for what it is—just plain bad luck. Just like the college football fan who said he wouldn't call for the coach's head after a losing streak. Rather than blame you for it, there is a greater chance that the public will see the second occurrence during the crisis in a more balanced context.

Think of the example of the popular yoga-wear company Lululemon.

In March 2013, the company announced a recall of black yoga pants, which had been manufactured and sold to women despite being too sheer—strike one. It was a big hit against the company, given there had been several recalls of Lululemon products adding to the notion that somehow the wildly successful retailer was cutting corners on quality. The stock price took a hit and Lululemon faced widespread media criticism. But the issue wouldn't go away. More concerns were raised throughout the spring and it was suddenly announced in June that CEO Christine Day would step down—strike two. Day called it a "personal decision."

Then fast forward to November when co-founders Chip and Shannon Wilson did a TV interview with Bloomberg. The interview was supposed to be about how to meditate in 60 seconds. But then host Trish Regan asked simply: "What's going on with the pants?" Chip Wilson started out by calling the issue "overblown," but then he went down with strike three, the last fatal blow. "Quite frankly, some women's bodies just actually don't work for it. . . . It is really about the rubbing through the thighs, how much pressure is there." Reaction was swift and damning. He was blaming women and their bodies for his own product's shortcomings. It was a full-blown crisis that threatened to devastate the Lululemon brand. Social media was ablaze with outrage. Chip Wilson made it worse the next day in a YouTube apology in which he talked about himself first, as opposed to the women he'd insulted. ABC's *Good Morning America* called it one of the worst apologies ever.[6] He reinforced the conditioned stereotype of a business tycoon who put his own self-interest ahead of the interests of his customers. And he completely failed to apologize to women, or to his customers, instead focusing his remarks on Lululemon employees.

Then it became about piling on, as it inevitably does. Several online petitions demanded his resignation. Media began reporting on Chip Wilson greatest-hits-style lists of his controversial quotes,[7] including that "most people live in a state of mediocrity"; a discussion of how the Japanese vocabulary has no "L" in it, so he deliberately set out to put three "Ls" in his company name Lululemon because "it's kind of funny to watch them try to say it"; and his infamous suggestion that breast cancer came to prominence in the 1990s "due to the number of cigarette-smoking power women who were on the pill . . . and taking on the stress previously left to men in the working world." One month later, Chip Wilson was gone from the company he created. He resigned as chairman of the board and also from his role as non-executive chairman. The company announced a new CEO to replace Day, and a new board chair to replace Wilson. Still, Lululemon faces a class action lawsuit brought by investors who claim the company inflated the value of its stock by failing to disclose, as required under securities law, the problems with the sheer yoga pants.

Clearly, after months of criticism, Wilson was feeling defensive. He lost focus on the interests of his customers. Instead, it was self-interest that brought him down.

Whole Foods' John Mackey, shared this advice. At the end of the day, leaders need to see a crisis as a gift; as an opportunity for personal growth. "If a crisis comes your way, you have an opportunity to learn and grow from it. Most people don't. Most people are damaged psychologically. Their self-esteem may be crippled. It may be something they never overcome. So I don't recommend it as a therapy for people, but if it does come your way you can use it as an opportunity to grow."

## Notes

1.   http://en.wikipedia.org/wiki/Walter_Bradford_Cannon
2.   http://cmhc.utexas.edu/stressrecess/Level_One/fof.html
3.   www.theglobeandmail.com/news/national/online-glitch-gives-brick-customers-50-discount-price-cut-wont-be-honoured/article16117544/
4.   http://business.time.com/2013/12/26/delta-glitch/
5.   http://sports.espn.go.com/ncf/news/story?id=4496615
6.   www.youtube.com/watch?v=u4jlBlTlkSk
7.   http://business.financialpost.com/2013/12/10/lululemon-athletica-chip-wilson-controversy/

# Chapter 4

# Organizational Paralysis

YOU CAN BE the world's most experienced crisis manager but if your organization doesn't understand what it will be like to manage a crisis —big decisions in small time frames, how counter-intuitive the process is, the need to shatter expectations—it is set up to fail every time. As Benjamin Franklin once said, "By failing to prepare, you are preparing to fail." But it's not just about having names on a crisis team organizational chart, or having a crisis protocol, or a hotline number set up and a crisis dark site ready to launch on the web. At the end of the day it is about some of the most fundamental aspects of organizational behavior, including the ability to speak truth to power. It is about whether an organization can take the long-term view even when it means short-term pain. And ultimately, it is about the leadership qualities of the CEO.

So where do organizations lose the crisis before it has even begun, from a behavioral point of view? The first gap in crisis management policy for most companies, government agencies, or other organizations is that, while they consider crisis preparation and protocol as important in theory, it's not important enough to do today. "Our people are just very busy right now." "Maybe we will have money to fund it next quarter." "We've really got to get to that soon." These are all comments crisis experts have heard many times. "It's just not a priority right now." There are some exceptions. A food manufacturer I have worked with holds a full-day crisis training session for its managers once a year that includes running through mock crisis responses and actions in simulated scenarios. Another client has quarterly crisis simulations that are conducted by staff from all departments. But for the most part, companies and organizations are caught flat-footed. Mid-level management isn't sure how their CEO will respond. Individual managers might consider crisis an area that has no upside for their own career trajectory, only a potential downside, so they take an exit ramp. In some organizations, there may be unresolved turf wars over jurisdiction. Whatever the reason, the lack of a protocol, planning, and training is the first ingredient in a recipe for disaster.

The lack of a protocol, planning, and training is the first ingredient in a recipe for disaster.

When a crisis does hit unexpectedly, it is alarming to witness how many organizations lapse into a form of paralysis in the critical early hours. It might be miscommunication, disorganization, lack of information, outdated traditions, obfuscation, wishful thinking that the crisis will quietly recede, or all of the above—but it adds up to organizational paralysis. Ohio State University's Leadership Center published its 11 Commandments of Organizational Paralysis years ago, but it still stands up very well today. It includes such gems as, "I wish it were that easy," "When you've been around a little while longer, you'll understand," and "How dare you suggest that what we are doing is wrong!" The shame of it is that most crises start with a relatively obvious warning, even in today's era when things move at the speed of light. Most large companies and organizations now monitor social media and mainstream media daily; even smaller companies who cannot afford such monitoring can set up emailed Google Alerts. Business offices tend to get complaint calls into their customer service desk or call center. The breakdown usually occurs at that fateful moment when someone in an organization tries to warn that there are signs of a developing crisis, but that warning is disregarded.

Now, to be fair, some crises are difficult to foresee. Even former Fed Chairman Alan Greenspan didn't see the 2008 mortgage meltdown and subsequent near-depression coming, which is hard to imagine, in hindsight. Sometimes more junior staff in an organization don't want to push their point when initially flagging a potential crisis because they don't want to be viewed as being negative, or lacking confidence. So, absent a proper crisis protocol, most organizations tend to fail at this moment of judgment. Either the volume with which the staff person flags the issue is too low, or his or her manager fails to recognize the threat level and doesn't escalate it. The process can still bog down above the manager's level with a supervisor or senior executive that chooses to hope the issue will go away. Another comment often heard in these situations is: "Nobody knows about this yet, by and large, so why should we put out a press release and make it into an issue? That's crazy." Some executives actually think they are doing their CEO a favor by not bringing them into the loop, allowing the CEO to—at some later time—rightfully deny that he or she was aware of the situation. That's why it is important for staff at every single level of your organization to understand crisis communications policies and procedures. If you plan to conduct training, as you should, you need to consider everyone from the person who answers the telephone to the CEO, and all the levels in between.

We've talked about what to expect in a crisis environment and also about the fight or flight response that will tend to cause us to react defensively. But in a surprising number of cases, companies don't react at all, at least not initially, due to this early paralysis. By the time they do react, it is too late. This is why organizational paralysis is so damaging. Sometimes it is a syndrome referred to as analysis paralysis, which involves the over-thinking of a situation so thoroughly and in such a time-consuming way that no action is ever taken.

But in my view, analysis paralysis is not a problem unique to crisis communications—organizations that suffer from analysis paralysis do so across the board, stifling creativity and impeding flexibility. The problem, in terms of crisis communications, is that by the time a company or organization reacts (late) when the crisis is underway, chances are good that it has already faced significant criticism. That criticism makes it even more likely that many people in the organization will react defensively. People tend to feel "wronged." They often turn to crisis experts like myself for help at this stage and what we inevitably hear is a version of: "How we're being treated is totally unfair. You need to make it stop."

## The Focus on Self-Interest

Now think about it. "You need to make it stop," is just a modified version of former BP CEO Tony Hayward's "I'd like my life back" comment. It focuses entirely on the self-interest of the organization ("How we're being treated . . .") as opposed to addressing the impacts the crisis is having on customers or the public. So you can see how, in this instance, the organization that is trying to manage the crisis finds itself in a position where it is already in a hole and it is still digging.

Early in 2014 when New Jersey Governor Chris Christie discovered (through media reports allegedly) that his chief of staff had ordered lane closures and resulting massive traffic jams—the so-called Bridgegate—to make life miserable for a New Jersey mayor who didn't support Christie's re-election strategy, the Governor held a 105-minute press conference in which he spoke about 20,000 words and apologized many times. Yet to some, all that effort was spoiled by the fact that Christie's comments were primarily positioned in his own self-interest, as opposed to the interests of hundreds of thousands of people who were unjustly wronged.

He talked about how "sad" he was and how "angry" he was. He talked about what had just happened *to him*. As writer Dana Milbank of the *Washington Post* noted in a column titled "New Jersey Narcissist" (Jan. 10, 2014), Christie kept talking about himself at this press conference, using the word *I* 692 times, *I'm* 119 times, *I've* 67 times, *me* 83 times and *my/myself* 134 times. As Milbank pointed out, Christie said he fired his chief of staff "because she lied to me," not because she ordered a traffic jam on the George Washington Bridge as payback against a political opponent.

Still, Christie did one thing that is a crisis communications best practice. He showed up. As the *de facto* CEO of New Jersey's state government, he stepped forward and owned the crisis. He vaporized any organizational paralysis that may have existed at the statehouse. Had that paralysis occurred, political pundits and social media commentators would have filled the vacuum, most with negative speculation. And so for stepping up, Christie drew widespread applause. This is what I call the Leadership Principle of crisis communications. It's not just that the buck stops with the CEO in a crisis, but in fact it starts with the CEO.

> It's not just that the buck stops with the CEO in a crisis, but in fact it starts with the CEO. Questions about crisis communications approaches should be at or near the top of any CEO recruitment interview.

Leaders of every company or organization in the public or private sector need to understand that they can never have an efficient and effective crisis communications protocol without their full engagement. Employees and management need to know where the CEO is on crisis communications policy. The board of directors needs to know too. This is critically important for boards to consider when they go through the CEO recruitment process, and questions about crisis communications approaches should be at or near the top of any CEO recruitment interview.

Just like we talked about how the brain triggers the fight or flight response, we can think of an organization's leader as the head on a body. How that "body" is regarded will be determined by the decisions made by its "head." There is no substitute. Organizational paralysis or analysis paralysis can exist at management levels below the CEO. When it does, it can be very difficult, if not impossible, to sort out. But the CEO, and usually the CEO alone, can put a stop to it.

Ultimately, if the CEO does not show up when this leadership is required, the vast majority of blame for the organizational failure is heaped upon that CEO. I have witnessed CEOs who mistakenly believe that their role in a crisis is to protect their senior management team or their employees. They think their job is to be a morale booster. They see a crisis as an opportunity to engender more loyalty among staff by being their greatest defender, someone who argues to journalists that these are hard-working people and the allegations have been blown out of proportion. Again, they take a position of self-interest as opposed to public interest.

## The Public Loves a Crisis and So Does the Media

Another reality we need to clearly face—and another reason why careers of CEOs are made, or ruined, during a major crisis—is that the mainstream media and our culture (including popular TV dramas and movies) portray crisis management as a sport, with winners and losers. Mainstream media increasingly cover not just the crisis, but do stories about how the crisis was, or was not, well managed. I have done dozens of interviews with journalists about how crises were handled, with regard to everyone from Tiger Woods to Toronto's infamous Mayor Rob Ford ("Yes I have smoked crack cocaine . . . probably in one of my drunken stupors." *Toronto Star,* Nov. 5, 2013)

The phenomenon isn't just limited to the mainstream media, or even to social media. I can recall being excited to hear that crisis communications icon Judy Smith had met with TV producer Shonda Rhimes and that Rhimes planned to do for crisis communications what she had done for hospitals with her TV drama *Grey's Anatomy.* The result, of course, was ABC's hit TV show *Scandal,* which was loosely based on Smith's own experiences. Media outlets and broadcasters like ABC do this because there is a public appetite. For the media, this is often a way to "keep a story alive" as journalists say, or extend it another day. Also, people love stories about winners and losers. And people increasingly expect to be told what is going on behind the scenes—not just why the plane didn't take off on time, but who made the decision and when, and why it wasn't communicated to them sooner.

There is a public appetite because in this online, hyper-connected, digital world we live in, the public has a greater expectation than ever before about the degree to which companies and organizations will be accountable and transparent—and how quickly it should happen. That reality, along with the fervor with which crisis communications is debated and commented about in social media, explains why young people tend to have a better handle on the subject. As one Penn State student said after hearing a lecture about crisis communications, she attended because ". . . it's something you'll eventually have to deal with . . . you need to be ready to handle things at a moment's notice."[1] What that means in generational terms is that CEOs might not be prepared or even understand the harsh judgments younger people will make about their company or organization based on how it reacts at a time of crisis. But the reality is that, increasingly, the judgment will be based as much on how the company communicates about the crisis as what the company actually does about the crisis.

## The Leadership Principle

Even when organizations finally do communicate, they often drop the ball by over-thinking or making fundamental errors that fail to follow the Leadership Principle of crisis communications. In early 2013, after Canada's national postal delivery service, Canada Post, had failed to deliver any mail whatsoever over the Christmas period for several weeks, the government-owned corporation repeatedly refused to make its CEO available to media who were demanding answers. Several angry homeowners had complained—loudly—in the media, and the story had "legs" (momentum) both in the mainstream media and on social media.

Going back to our rule about wearing your customer's shoes when you consider your response, Canada Post made a bad situation worse when it violated the Leadership Principle by trying to tell people where the buck stopped. Most people who missed checks, Christmas cards, and other important mail (and didn't know why or when mail delivery would resume) felt like the buck stopped with the CEO, particularly at a crown corporation owned by Canadian taxpayers. And yet when the *Toronto Star* newspaper objected to Canada Post's CEO being absent, Canada Post senior vice president of delivery and customer experience made the horrible decision to try to teach the reporter a lesson. "The delivery of mail is my accountability. The buck stops here. It's me you should be dealing with." (*Toronto Star,* Jan. 10, 2014) This of course, created the inevitable outcome that the *Star* made an even bigger deal about the AWOL CEO. Never tell reporters who they should or should not interview. That is their job. Your job is to respond to the interview request. Or you may decide to decline the request. But *do not*, under any circumstances, explain to reporters how to do their job. That is one of the most fundamental rules of media relations.

Never tell reporters who they should or should not interview.

In terms of crisis communications, here is an organization that failed to communicate initially (organizational paralysis), then likely held a large and lengthy meeting to decide what to do after media revealed the problem (analysis paralysis, causing further delays), and against the Leadership Principle of crisis communications decided to try to get away with having a vice president be the face of the crisis.

Predictably, the strategy blew up, and it became about where the CEO was. A newspaper headline shouted: "Canada Post CEO Remains Silent on Delivery Delays." At least two customers quoted in the story said the CEO owed them answers. And he did. It's worth noting, of course, that once a story goes sideways like this, it opens the floodgates for others to speculate in mainstream media and on social media as to why the CEO is AWOL. One Member of Parliament even suggested to the *Star* that Canada Post was hiding its CEO because he had recently performed poorly in a public appearance when he shockingly suggested senior citizens would enjoy "super-mailboxes" (as opposed to home delivery) because it would offer them some exercise. That just suggested to the public that this was an organization in disarray, with weak leadership at the very top. Not the type of message you want to see communicated to people at the height of your crisis.

When it comes to CEOs and the Leadership Principle, there has been much debate in Public Relations and Crisis Communications circles about having a process to determine whether the CEO of an organization needs to comment publicly or not during a crisis. "Let's just put one of our VPs out there." Some experts have provided checklists and guides to walk you through the process of how to decide whether to have your CEO comment, or whether to keep him or her bottled up in some back room. The theory behind these guides is that by having a CEO comment, you may make the mistake of "elevating" the crisis rather than calming it down. I just can't state strongly enough how much I disagree with this approach. This kind of behavior doesn't shatter the public's negative expectations; it reinforces them.

To me, the Leadership Principle is absolute. Trying to measure when a CEO should be available and when he or she should not is like trying to measure how fast you could drive your car without wearing a seatbelt, then have a head-on collision, and not fly head-first through your windshield. It just makes no sense whatsoever. If a crisis is a small one, and is largely solved from a public interest or customer perspective, regardless of whether the CEO speaks out, it will go away because there is nothing left; there is no negative outcome left and no threat of a negative outcome. Problem solved. So why take the seatbelt risk? Why risk that your crisis will grow and magnify from a small one to a much bigger one that becomes about the behavior of your organization, and the "hiding" of your CEO? Is that worth it?

In fact, I would argue that there is no crisis too small for a CEO to be involved with, time allowing. Think of the football coach who unexpectedly paid the fan's invoice. Even when one customer is negatively impacted, that outreach from a CEO says a lot about your brand and those are the kinds of stories that go viral on social media. At the very least,

> There is no crisis too small for a CEO to be involved with.

even in the case of a small crisis, mainstream media or customers who see a CEO's immediate involvement often attribute positive leadership qualities to that involvement—"Boy he/she was really on top of it." I am not arguing for you to blow up the process with which you manage things like customer complaints. There are people who make a pastime of complaining about products solely in anticipation of receiving some kind of discount coupon in response. But once a situation has been determined to be a crisis for your organization, no matter how big or small, your CEO needs to be involved.

*Note*

1.  http://m.collegian.psu.edu/news/campus/article_3e1d48d4-3608-11e3-b620-0019bb30f31a.html?mode=jqm

# Chapter 5

# Crisis? What Crisis?

CRISIS COMMUNICATIONS PROTOCOLS are effective, but how do we know when to trigger them? There are wide ranging opinions about how to determine what is, or is not, an actual crisis. And that determination is so often what bedevils organizations and companies. When do you know? What is a justifiable reaction? What is an over-reaction? What about our stock? What will the Board say?

It's more of an art than a science. It is also impacted by many environmental elements lurking all around you, some of which may not be initially apparent. And remember, the closer you are to a company or an organization, the more blood, sweat, and tears you have poured into it, the less you will be able to imagine the sort of attacks that can develop and be leveled at you, as opposed to a dispassionate communications expert who is a step removed and who has years of experience in evaluating these threats. That is why it is always wise, when it comes to crisis communications policy and ongoing decision making, to have the benefit of outside crisis counsel.

Ultimately, this determination of a crisis—yes or no—is one of the most fascinating aspects of crisis management. Many times an event will occur that we think will develop into a major crisis and it never does; other times matters that seem fairly innocuous spiral out of control with unexpected and unanticipated twists and turns to become the gripping crisis we never imagined. But there are ways to level off these over-expectations and under-anticipations. Organizations can adopt policies that flatten the risk curve and lead to more predictable outcomes. After all, most crisis communications experts, myself included, would prefer that we make ourselves redundant because our clients became so adept at managing issues that they don't require our services.

To get there, we need to start thinking about "crisis avoidance" before we think about crisis management. Some refer to this as "issues management" since it comes prior to the crisis, and in some cases can avert the crisis. The best crises—if there are such beasts—are the ones that never get to the full-blown stage, but instead are effectively managed and serve as enhancers to your brand's reputation. When this becomes a repeatable process, it makes the determination of whether something should be defined as a crisis or not less relevant, since the same steps are being followed in each instance regardless of your expectations.

Each case becomes an "issues management file." So ultimately, what we are striving for is not an on-off switch that we flip for a crisis, but in fact, a set of policies and procedures that escalate when it comes to issues that potentially threaten your organization's reputation or business model, or potentially your personal reputation as a leader. In the meantime, by proactively dealing with issues that have caused some difficulty for your customers or stakeholders, you are building a stronger reputation for your brand that will hopefully serve as a sort of safety restraint airbag for the crash of the big head-on crisis, when it hits.

After all, there is no foolproof way to avoid a full-blown crisis. Issues management can tackle most of the situations that could develop into crises if not managed properly. But there is always the potential that a major crisis you could never have anticipated could strike. In that case, you won't have any difficulty identifying it as a crisis because it will be extremely unexpected and it will involve some combination of health and safety risks for your customers or employees, some form of alleged criminal activity or wrongdoing, or a tragic event. That is the sort of catastrophic crisis that is hard to miss. For the other issues that we can deal with proactively, we have issues management.

Effective issues management has little to do with crisis policy, per se, but actually relates to some of the most basic principles of communications—government relations, stakeholder relations, customer relations, and employee relations. Some communications advisers will spend very little time on these issues and instead focus on the (seemingly far sexier) crisis management topics. They will pull you into a room and say: "Okay, let's spend two days writing a press release about every potential crisis we think the company could face." That will result in a lot of valuable time being eaten up by members of your team writing and editing media materials that you will probably never use. And it puts the cart before the horse. It's like saying, "Let's talk about the Persian rugs for the family room," before you've even decided on the bricks, mortar, framing, electrical system, and roof for your new house. It just doesn't make any sense.

## Build Your Relationships

Just as everyone knows that football games are won at the line of scrimmage, your company is not likely to win at crisis communications without having strong and basic "blocking and tackling" programs in place on an ongoing basis that allow you to effectively communicate with employees, with customers, with suppliers and stakeholders, and with relevant government officials. These are the people who know your business and who will be watching closely when something goes wrong. For years I have been talking to clients about looking at these relationships like you would a bank account. When was the last time you made a deposit by building the relationship? Where is my balance with stakeholder X? These will be the people who are the first to notice if you don't seem to be in control during a crisis, and the people who others will reach out to in order to find out more information about you—so that's when you want to be able to make withdrawals from that relationship bank account. You want those stakeholders to reflect confidence in your organization and your leadership. Nothing is worse than having a journalist call a recognized leader in Sector Y, or a government official or local elected political representative, about your crisis, only to have that leader say: "I have no idea who these people are or how they do business." It makes your organization appear less credible and it tends to translate into open season on your reputation as the crisis unfolds.

That is why the first step in an effective issues management program is knowing who your stakeholders are and building those relationships and building links in your community. Do you have Corporate Social Responsibility (CSR) programs in place? How are you sharing that information? Have you done something innovative with your employees in terms of training or other Human Resources policies, say, for example, flex hours to help with the problem of traffic gridlock in your city? Does your CEO speak to college and university graduating classes about starting their careers?

> The first step in an effective issues management program is knowing who your stakeholders are.

There are many ways to build these stakeholder relationships and communicate your organization's values in a way that doesn't involve trying to get a reporter to write a media story. And there are many who have studied these policies around the world who would tell you that building solid stakeholder relationships is actually a more important element of your overall corporate communications strategy than crisis communications strategies. The *Journal of Public Relations Research,* a peer-reviewed academic journal, published an important paper in 2010 called "Organization-Public Relationships and Crisis Response Strategies: Impact on Attribution of Responsibility." It found: "People with a positive relationship with the organization were less likely to place blame for the crisis on the organization regardless of crisis response strategy."

Given that we have already mixed enough metaphors in this chapter, let's forget, for now, about the so-called "secret sauce" of crisis communications. It starts with basic and not-so-glamorous Communications 101 work. Without effectively managing in all those fundamental areas, no amount of crisis communications genius is going to help you get through unscathed.

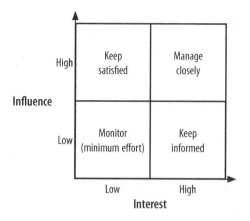

Let's start with stakeholder relations. For our purposes, let's define stakeholders as broadly including customers, government officials (municipal, state/provincial and federal), officials in your sector (public or private), regulatory bodies, and community officials. Stakeholders can also include "neighbors" in terms of businesses and others physically located near you—bankers/investors, insurance companies, law enforcement, unions, sector competitors, critics, environmental stakeholders, charities, religious or ethnic organizations, or other influential individuals or entities. As you would with any communications initiative, to measure success when you implement a stakeholder relations program you need to do a baseline measurement up front. You need to identify where you are currently through a process of stakeholder mapping. The most commonly used process is the four-quadrant[1] stakeholder map above.

To begin, it's best to understand how this map works and what its purpose is. In short, it allows you to measure where your organization stands today with stakeholders, strategize about where you want to be within a defined time frame, and what you need to do to get there. Mapping is best done by a third party agency. Most PR or reputation management firms can walk you through this process and conduct it for you. It involves fairly in-depth interviews with key stakeholders that you will identify—both positive and negative—to be part of this qualitative research.

Based on these interviews, your stakeholders are then mapped in the four-quadrant grid, with the left vertical being power, from low rising to high power, and the bottom horizontal being support, from low on the left to high support on the right. Each of the quadrants identifies a stakeholder by characteristics that emerge from the research and also maps that stakeholder in relation to other stakeholders. In other words, they aren't just dropped in—even within the high power group you would mark the most powerful stakeholder in the highest position near the top bar, and other high powers slightly below. As becomes apparent in discussions you will have about how this looks, companies typically don't spend much time on low power, low support stakeholders.

## Powerful Stakeholders

Your priority initially is maintaining strong relationships with, or strengthening relationships with, stakeholders in the upper right quadrant because they are not only the most influential, they are the most supportive of what you are trying to do. For example, if you were a community leader trying to persuade your city government to install speed bumps on the streets surrounding the elementary school on your neighborhood, local police officers who supported you would likely be in that upper right quadrant—both influential (because of their experience in law enforcement) and highly supportive (as promoters of community safety). The school board officials, who know that the city is going to charge them for the cost of the speed bumps, might be in the upper left quadrant, as highly influential but low in terms of interest and support, possibly because they already pay the expense of crossing guards on those streets to safely monitor children crossing the road. A taxpayer protection group might be in the bottom left quadrant, unsupportive of spending more taxpayer dollars to install speed bumps but not very influential on the issue because the group typically opposes all sorts of expenditures that could drive taxes up.

Ultimately, the stakeholder relations program you design after this mapping exercise has the strategic objective of moving important stakeholders from one quadrant to the next, or solidifying them within the quadrant so as to protect yourself from the possibility that they could suddenly become unsupportive. You are asking yourself: What are we doing right to earn the high support of these powerful stakeholders in the upper right quadrant and what do we have to do to maintain that support? Next, you look at the upper left quadrant and the lower right. In upper left, we have powerful stakeholders who do not support us very much. Can we move them to the right by increasing their support for us? If so, what is the best way to do that? What would it take to move them from the upper left to the upper right? Since these are powerful folks, this should be a priority. Secondly, we know that in the bottom right quadrant we have people who support us enthusiastically but are not very influential. What can we do to help them increase their power and influence? Can we partner with them in some way? There are good options for addressing that. Next you would decide how you planned to contact or interact with these people and organizations to move them within a specified time frame. At the end of that period—perhaps a year, in some cases in two or three years—you would do it all again by re-interviewing and re-mapping your stakeholders.

Getting back to that stakeholder bank account we talked about. Implementing the stakeholder relations plan amounts to making those deposits proactively. Well managed, your stakeholders represent a healthy balance on a rainy day who will back you up at times of crisis. They lend credibility to your organization's remedial actions and the intentions you communicate publicly. And given the pervasiveness of public cynicism, you will need these withdrawals at a time of crisis—"take me at my word" might not be good enough. So don't get so distracted by short-term business goals or organizational objectives that you neglect this important area of investment.

I won't take you through effective government relations, or internal employee communications, or customer marketing communications—those are disciplines that are well-explored elsewhere and require, in my view, the engagement of experts in those areas. It is important to understand that when you have effective two-way channels functioning in all these areas, you flatten the curve of needing to make an absolute declaration about whether an issue constitutes a crisis or not. That's because you will be engaged with your employees on an ongoing basis and will hear back promptly from them in ways that may help flag a crisis. It also means that your employees are less likely to lose confidence in your company or organization when the crisis hits; and that your efforts to retain high-value employees are enhanced. Some people talk about listening to the "wind in the trees" to tell of a coming storm. Listen to your customers when they register concern. Keep those channels of communication open at all times. Be where your customers are on social media.

Make no mistake, considerable hard work, diligence, thoughtfulness, and experience will be required. One of the greatest mistakes in the crisis communications world is that people endlessly study and evaluate how a crisis was handled once it struck; or they endlessly study how organizations recovered after a crisis. But you seldom see studies or discussions about what an organization did before the crisis and how that impacted its ability to manage during the crisis. In this sense, pre-crisis work, or issues management, is not the responsibility of a few select individuals, but instead requires a total team effort. You will need your Human Resources people as much as you need your Marketing people; you will need your Government Relations people and Corporate Communications staff.

I am of the firm belief that your Government Relations and Media Relations groups need to be joined at the hip—politicians don't like surprises; they don't like being asked questions about issues your company has raised that they haven't been briefed about. If there is a crisis in your sector, and the elected politician responsible for your sector gets hit by the media flat-footed because you failed to brief him or her, you can bet the government will treat you just a tad more harshly than it otherwise would have. That is just human nature. On the other hand, a political leader in charge of, say, food safety, can help contain a crisis if, when asked about your food manufacturing contamination issue, that politician has been provided (by you) with key messages about the steps already being taken to ensure safety. When you do give key government figures a "heads up" in advance, as a courtesy, before you go out with something to the media, that creates goodwill in the relationship.

## Importance of Employees

And one final point about these stakeholder groups. When you are facing a crisis head on, it's important to prioritize your stakeholders in terms of who you will communicate with first. But never, ever, let your employees learn a major piece of information or a significant development through the media. Tell them first yourself. We will explore this in great detail later on. Once you start to lose the support of your employees, it becomes a very slippery downhill slope for your organization—particularly since in many crisis scenarios they are the people you will be counting on to do the actual work required to turn the situation around and re-establish order and safety.

> Never, ever, let your employees learn a major piece of information or a significant development through the media.

So what does proactive stakeholder relations and issues management look like? The Issues Management Council gave the prestigious W. Howard Chase Award for excellence in issues management to DuPont in 2013 for its project *Food Security: Welcome to the Global Collaboratory.* Facing legislative and public opinion opposition on the issue of genetically modified foods, DuPont set out to champion the issue of food security, noting the world's population will grow from 7 billion to 9 billion people by the year 2050, resulting in a fierce competition among countries to feed their citizens unless more sustainable food production policies are adopted.

DuPont acknowledged controversy over the issue of genetically modified foods and also that about 40 percent of the company's $35 billion in annual revenues comes from agriculture and food security. In 2010, it announced the creation of the *The DuPont Advisory Committee on Agriculture Innovation and Productivity for the 21st Century,* chaired by former Senator Tom Daschle. That committee researched policy options and issued a public report in 2011. The following year, DuPont worked with *The Economist* to develop the *Global Food Security Index,* which assesses and ranks 105 countries in terms of food security factors such as affordability, accessibility, nutrition, and safety. When the index was unveiled, more than 3,000 government officials, business leaders, representatives of non-governmental organizations and academics attended events in Washington, Brussels, Sao Paulo, Santiago, and Johannesburg. The event was also live-streamed on the internet.

Remember the four-quadrant stakeholder map we discussed? DuPont conducted what it called an "Influencer Quotient Mapping" project that analyzed both individuals and organizations in terms of their level of influence and opinion about food security issues. Now, unless your company or organization also has $35 billion in annual revenues, and few do, this example will seem like an extreme example—or at least an extremely expensive one. But think about what DuPont did here. It staked out a global leadership position on a vital issue. It acknowledged its interest in this issue. And it involved thousands of stakeholders in the process. Is it any wonder that one financial journalist wrote an article in 2013 about two similar chemical companies entitled: "Why Is Monsanto Evil, But DuPont Isn't?"[2] The GMO food controversy continues, but instead of being reactive, DuPont is out ahead of the issue, communicating from a position of strength and credibility.

Ultimately, there are no shortcuts. Be wary of those who would tell you that there is a formula you can apply that determines whether something is a crisis or not. As we've talked about before, the web is riddled with "The Top 10 Ways to Tell if You Are in a Crisis" or "Ask Yourself These 5 Questions When You Think a Crisis Has Struck." Avoid these vapid oversimplifications. They are the Ginsu steak knives of crisis communications. There is only one rule and it is: There are no rules.

Usually the people peddling these to-do lists are only interested in selling you a product. They're not as interested in whether you have a good outcome, or not, when the crisis hits. For that you need a partner who stands shoulder to shoulder with you and your team and who has the necessary experience and judgment to adapt quickly to changing circumstances. If you have an existing PR agency relationship, ask them about their crisis communications capabilities, or whether they work with a third party specialist.

In the United States you can check with the local branch of the PRSA (Public Relations Society of America) for recommendations on crisis communications specialists, while in Canada the CPRS (Canadian Public Relations Society) is a good resource. And finally, you can also check with leaders from other organizations as to who they trust in this area. The big multi-national PR firms all offer comprehensive crisis communications programs, including FleishmanHillard, Edelman, Weber Shandwick, and Hill+Knowlton. Many skilled crisis experts have also gone out on their own, or formed smaller boutique firms. My advice is to try to find someone in your area who also understands the local political climate and brings some longstanding media and stakeholder relationships to the table.

There are so many variables that it is extremely difficult to categorize crises. Over 30 years in media and communications I have seen endless examples of crises that each have unique elements. This is also what people find so fascinating and what draws so many students of communications to crisis work; almost every crisis is different and just when you think you have seen them all, something comes along that is even more of an eye opener.

## Effective Management Can Shorten a Crisis (or Not)

Sometimes a crisis appears on the face of it to be a crippling one—but is so effectively managed that the issue is surprisingly short-lived and the brand carries on largely unaffected. This happened with Domino's Pizza, as described by Vice President of Communications Tim McIntyre in an interview with PRSA.[3] When staff at a North Carolina store videotaped themselves in 2009 putting cheese up their noses and doing other disgusting things to a sandwich and then posted the video on YouTube, it could have been devastating for the brand. It was a food marketer's nightmare. Within a few days more than 1 million people had viewed the disturbing video. But McIntyre and the Dominos team got their CEO engaged right off the bat, tracked down the perpetrators, buttoned down their social media strategy, and dealt with the issue straight on. McIntyre told PRSA that although there was an extraordinary spike in chatter about Dominos, the spike plummeted right back down to normal levels within the same short amount of time—largely due to how well the issue was handled.

On the flip side, a crisis that some might think could have been dealt with easily—before it spiraled out of control in 2000—was the crisis involving Firestone tires and Ford.[4] There was a spike in Ford SUV rollovers that seemed to be caused either by the design of the trucks, or by the fact that the Firestone tires they were equipped with kept blowing due to tread separation. More than 100 people were killed and thousands more seriously injured in the crashes. But rather than getting to the bottom of the issue and communicating about how they were going to fix it, Ford and Firestone blamed each other. It became an orgy of self-interest that dragged both companies down. Firestone said it was a Ford design problem and error in tire inflation instructions to vehicle owners; Ford claimed the Firestone tread ply design was to blame.

This settled nothing and the crisis became sustained, so much so, that it led to a Senate investigation that heard about "a documented cover-up by Ford and Firestone."[5] It got so ugly, and went on so long, that the Firestone CEO finally sent a letter to the head of Ford severing their business relationship—one that had endured more than 100 years. It was stunning to witness the degree to which this crisis spiraled out of control, given that it could have been effectively managed if the two companies had done the right thing and focused immediately on the public interest. Think about it—the crisis was still going strong a year after it erupted. Sales plummeted for both companies—Firestone was later forced to shut down a manufacturing plant. The two companies were described in *The Baltimore Sun* (Sept. 17, 2009) at the time as being in "free fall" over circumstances that needn't have happened.

That length of sustained crisis is almost unheard of today. Contrast that to the speedy and widespread General Motors recalls of 2014 and it's easy to see how the climate in that sector has changed when it comes to safety recalls. I cannot stress it enough—forget about crisis communications lists and ask yourself these questions: Is what we're saying and doing focused on the public interest? Are we shattering public expectations as we fix this? Or is our reaction really wrapped up in our own self-interest?

## Notes

1. http://mutuals.cabinetoffice.gov.uk/how/stakeholder-map
2. www.investopedia.com/articles/investing/061913/why-monsanto-evil-dupont-isnt.asp
3. https://www.prsa.org/Intelligence/TheStrategist/Articles/view/8226/102/Domino_s_delivers_during_crisis_The_company_s_step#.Uztl_a1dVDp
4. http://content.time.com/time/business/article/0,8599,128198,00.html
5. http://dcomm.cxc.lsu.edu/portfolios/09spr/dcoron1/BridgestoneFirestoneCaseStudy.pdf

# Chapter 6

# The Decider: The CEO

"I'M THE DECIDER and I decide what's best," former President George W. Bush famously said in 2006, referring to his continued confidence in then-Defense Secretary Donald Rumsfeld, whose resignation had been called for at the time by six retired military generals. I covered President Bush's inauguration and his administration in those early months, through the attacks of 9/11 and until just shortly after the one-year anniversary of those attacks in Fall 2002. I am eternally grateful to President Bush for this quote for reasons that I will discuss in this chapter. But before we dive into that, his defense of Rumsfeld is a reminder to all of us of another famous media quote that relates to the unpredictability of crisis communications.

There were a lot of great quotes to be had during that Bush administration, but journalists and PR professionals around the world still love to recall the "unknown unknowns" soliloquy that Rumsfeld famously delivered in a Pentagon briefing (which I covered) in February 2002. The quote appears in the movie *Zero Dark Thirty*, became the title of Rumsfeld's own memoir (made into the 2013 documentary titled *The Unknown Known*), and, in short, is one of the most famous and talked about quotes of modern times. In the event it is "unknown" to you, here is the full quote as he said it: "[Media] Reports that say that something hasn't happened are always interesting to me, because as we know, there are known knowns; there are things we know that we know. There are known unknowns; that is to say, there are things that we now know we don't know. But there are also unknown unknowns—there are things we do not know we don't know."[1]

The real debate about crisis communications would be whether is it a "known unknown"—that is, we know we are likely going to face a crisis at some point, we just don't know exactly what it will be; or whether crises are "unknown unknowns"—in other words we cannot possibly know if or when a crisis will strike, nor what that crisis will be. But one thing is for certain: When it does happen, we know we will need The Decider.

When I think about "the decider" I think about those PR professionals who believe that involving the CEO just exacerbates the crisis. I disagree. The only reason to keep a CEO on the sidelines is because the issue is too minor—you simply cannot call in the CEO every time you have a small issue to manage. These are leaders with severe time constraints. You want to deploy them strategically for maximum effect.

On the other hand, a CEO in this celebrity era we live in remains the face of many companies: Marissa Mayer at Yahoo, Sheryl Sandberg at Facebook, Meg Whitman at Hewlett Packard, Jeff Bezos at Amazon, Warren Buffett at Berkshire Hathaway, to name a few. Look at the resurrection of the Yahoo brand (and stock) after Mayer took over. Yahoo didn't get that much better overnight. But the cult of Mayer's personality and reputation delivered higher expectations for services and innovation from Yahoo.

Ideally your CEO is already driving your company or organization's reputation through various channels including social media and stakeholder relations; therefore having that person involved in a significant crisis should not surprise the media or the public. On the contrary, there is a trend today more than ever before—even on mid-level crises that do not involve deaths, alleged criminal activity, or major financial repercussions—for the public and media to expect CEOs to be fully engaged and call them out when they are not.

## The CEO Engagement Scorecard

The December 2013 ice storm that struck Central and Eastern Canada and the Northeastern United States provided a classic illustration of this expectation. A total of 600,000 households were plunged into darkness and cold when the power grid was knocked out by downed power lines and blown transformers in Toronto and the surrounding area. If that wasn't bad enough, the first week of January brought a vicious cold snap—weather so cold that Toronto's Pearson International Airport ceased operations. Then it was learned that the national postal service, Canada Post, had failed to deliver mail—any mail—to several parts of the Toronto region, home to more than 6 million people.

Here were three organizations—Toronto Hydro, Pearson International Airport (the Greater Toronto Airport Authority), and Canada Post—and three CEOs who each took a different approach. So it was, perhaps, not surprising that Canada's largest newspaper, the *Toronto Star,* wrote an article grading the three CEOs for how they handled the crises. Anthony Haines, CEO of Toronto Hydro, held daily press conferences—for 10 straight days—and answered any and all questions about the ice storm power outages. He was graded an "A" in the article based on the input of three crisis communications professionals, myself included. Howard Eng, CEO of the airport, was missing in action for three days while people slept on his airport floor, all the while living in a furiously frustrating information vacuum about their travel plans that was well-documented by TV cameras. He was said to have been in Calgary "on business" but no one at the airport could explain what that business was, or why he could not be reached. Eng eventually surfaced, apologized, and announced a review would be conducted of what had happened. He was scored a "C" because he did eventually appear and addressed the issues. The Canada Post CEO, Deepak Chopra, was scored a failing "F" grade.

Media Report Card:

Anthony Haines, CEO, Toronto Hydro, held daily press conferences for 10 straight days: **A**

Howard Eng, CEO, Pearson Intl. Airport, was missing in action for three days: **C**

Deepak Chopra, Canada Post CEO, AWOL: **F**

He was AWOL much longer than Eng. Members of Parliament began to speculate that Canada Post was keeping its CEO hidden because he was such a poor communicator—it generated wave after wave of negative media coverage and scorching hot negativity on social media.

And by the way—in terms of accountability and public expectations, it is worth noting that the newspaper article specified the salaries of all three CEOs, so that readers could further judge the value they delivered. The only one of the three CEOs who shattered the public's expectations was Haines. He wasn't a well-known figure prior to the storm, but he quickly became a trusted voice. His company's email, telephone, and online customer feedback systems all crashed during the ice storm, which made his daily presence even more critical. He acknowledged that many people could not get in touch with his organization and he pledged to do better. When he didn't have the answer for people about when their power would come back on, he said so. He calmly explained exactly what his work crews were doing and what the priority sequencing would be to restore power, even when it meant he was telling some customers that they would have to wait several more days to get their power back, in some cases until after Christmas Day. There was never any sense that Haines knew more than he was saying and few second-guessed Toronto Hydro's handling of the crisis. This wasn't what some call positive "PR spin." In fact it was actually disheartening news for many not to know when their heat would be restored. It was a great example of shattering that ingrained public expectation that an electrical utility is a giant bureaucracy designed to collect bills and not be very responsive to customers. Here was the face of the company, expressing his regret, explaining the process in a detailed way, even looking exhausted after he'd gone days without any sleep. People could relate to him.

I have always found it curious that some PR professionals would counsel against involving a CEO as the spokesperson in a serious crisis situation. Think about it. Many companies that do not have a crisis plan in place when struck by a disastrous crisis are soon out of business. Even those that survive and rebuild often see sweeping change brought to the executive suite—so the CEO you are protecting today likely won't have a job tomorrow. There's no sense protecting your CEO's job if there is no job and no company left to lead.

Not to mention the fact that protecting the CEO is exactly the type of self-interested behavior that gets companies into so much trouble. How is it in the public interest that a CEO's vacation is not interrupted to deal with a crisis? How is it in the public interest to try to strategically have another executive be the fall guy and face of the crisis? These are very self-interested calculations. No matter how smart your PR advisers think they are, the public is smarter. The public will see through it every time, particularly in conversations on social media sites like Twitter. As they say, "It's not the crime, it's the cover-up." Part of what is counter-intuitive about effective crisis management is the use of the CEO. In most cases, the CEO didn't personally make the manufacturing error, or the technical malfunction, or even the error in judgment. He or she is not directly responsible. But the CEO does represent the company. The CEO sets expectations for the company's behavior. And the CEO is the person with whom the public believes the buck stops.

## Get Ahead of the Crisis

The gold standard in crisis managements is the infamous Tylenol tampering crisis. Back in 1982 someone injected cyanide into some packages of Tylenol, killing seven people. The company, Johnson and Johnson, acted swiftly. CEO James Burke appeared at news conferences and in TV commercials explaining that a stunning 31 million capsules of Tylenol were being recalled at a cost of $31 us million. Burke quickly developed tamper-proof packaging that remains an industry standard today, and the brand Tylenol recovered and has continued to prosper.

In the summer of 2007 toy maker Mattel, which had already been hit with recalls due to issues about products exported from China, faced two more federal recalls in one week. CEO Robert Eckert had a staff of 16 PR people personally telephone the 40 largest media outlets in the United States. On the day when the story broke, he did 14 TV interviews and another 20 interviews by telephone. Within the week Mattel had done interviews with more than 300 media outlets, and CEO Eckert was the face of the crisis for the company, which was lauded by parents and media for being straightforward about the crisis and what it was doing to fix it.

The theory behind getting out ahead of a crisis the way Mattel did was memorably captured by Yale-educated lawyer Lanny Davis, who was recruited to work in the Clinton White House. Davis, who helped Clinton with the Monica Lewinsky scandal, coined the phrase "Tell it all, tell it early, tell it yourself," that has taken on almost biblical proportions in the crisis communications world. Davis, who is still widely sought via his Washington law firm Lanny J. Davis and Associates, was essentially arguing in favor of getting truthful information about yourself out first, by yourself, even if it is damaging to you. Again, his theory, on the face of it, represents the opposite of self-interest. Who would call public attention to their own failings? But it is a lesson well-learned by those, like Davis, who are experienced in crisis management. And to do it properly, you really do need the CEO out front and center.

Which brings us to a fundamental principle about the Decider. When a crisis strikes, it is a time when members of an organization need to speak truth to power. If you are a leader, you need to make it clear to your employees that they can speak the truth to you—that you expect them to do so—and that there will be no repercussions. And if you are a senior manager in a company or organization, you need to be bold and speak the truth to your bosses even when you feel intimidated by them. This is not the time for internal politicking. Every morsel of information is critically essential. Every viewpoint and perspective needs to be on the table.

As we've said with regard to well-intentioned executives who would try to shield their CEO from a crisis—don't do him or her any favors that will turn out to be the opposite and actually put your CEO's future at risk. If you see leaders in your organization headed down the wrong path, a self-interested path, call them out. It is your duty. You have a responsibility to express what you believe to be true, even if you have concerns that there could be painful or embarrassing consequences. Doing what's right will always be the right thing. And if there is a person in a position of power over you who reacts during a crisis by punishing you for delivering information or standing on principle, that person is likely doomed to fail because his or her approach is entirely wrong-headed. A good CEO or leader doesn't want to be surrounded by people who always say "yes." He or she wants to be challenged. Good leaders don't just hear what they want to hear, they demand to know what they need to hear. They want the facts and they want the options for action, including the options that may be uncomfortable, or even painful, to contemplate. A workplace rife with intimidation and extreme hierarchy is a workplace that is ripe to fail spectacularly when a crisis hits because internal communications—real and honest communications between employees at all levels—is virtually nonexistent.

One thing is certain: How a company or organization manages a crisis will reveal how functional or dysfunctional the management structure is. Ideally, the senior leadership will foster an environment of trust at a time of crisis. To avoid being caught in the perception of a cover-up, leaders need to draw information out of employees, including even the smallest, most obscure tidbits. Employees must never be left with the perception that somehow they are doing something heroic if they cover up a fact that would obscure the real reason why a crisis or tragic event occurred. Quite the opposite. Employees must know that they can come forward with information without any fear of retribution.

> How a company or organization manages a crisis will reveal how functional or dysfunctional the management structure is.

There is a growing consensus that it is no longer possible for CEOs to remain safely tucked behind closed boardroom doors. The social media leadership branding agency BRANDfog issued a global CEO report in 2014 after surveying 1,000 employees in the U.S. and U.K. who worked for a range of companies from start-ups to Fortune 1,000 companies. The report concluded that between 2012 and 2013 the perception that C-level executives who participated on social media were better leaders increased from 45 percent to 75 percent; as well a majority of respondents in the U.S. and U.K. felt those leaders were more trustworthy; and a majority felt that social media was an absolutely essential tool for C-level executives at a time of crisis. Ann Charles, the founder of BRANDfog, summed it up: "In today's hyper-connected, information-driven world, CEOs and senior executives alike are expected to have an active social presence. Brand image, brand trust, and a company's long-term success depend on it."[2]

**2013–2014**
Perception that C-level executives who participated on social media were better leaders:
↑ 35%

Number of CEOs of major corporations with Twitter accounts:
5 – 6%

CEOs with no social media presence at all:
68%

Still, despite the trend analysis, the number of CEOs of major corporations who had a Twitter account in 2014 numbered in the single digits at around 5 or 6 percent.[3] A study by CEO.com showed that during that same time period about 68 percent of CEOs had no social media presence or activity at all.[4] One of the most actively social CEOs in North America is someone I have worked with, the CEO of Canada's Tangerine bank (formerly ING Direct) Peter Aceto, who told Forbes.com (Jan. 30, 2013) that social media is the new yardstick for leaders. "Successful leaders will no longer be measured just by stock price," Aceto said. "Managing and communicating with shareholders, employees, government, community, customers will be table stakes in the future. They are talking about your business anyway. Why not be included in the conversation?"

Still, a 2012 report by the PR firm Weber Shandwick showed that many CEOs who do not participate in social media felt it was too unusual for their sector, that there was no return on the investment of their time, or that it was still too risky.[5] However, progress is being made. Mary Barra, the new CEO of General Motors, used her @mtbarra Twitter account to communicate on the GM ignition switch recall issue, which became the subject of hearings before Congress. For example, she posted: "We're working hard to resolve the @GM ignition switch recall. I answer some of your questions in these videos:" followed by a link to GM's consumer-friendly *FastLane* web page.[6] The videos, which also link to GM's YouTube channel, have Barra delivering some very personal messages in an authentic way. "When they presented these to me," Barra said of interim solutions, "the very first question I asked is: Would you let your family, your spouse, your children, drive these vehicles in this condition? And they said yes."

Barra's efforts are a strong bellwether of the social transparency consumers increasingly expect. Ernst and Young captured this trend in its 2013 report *The Journey Toward Greater Customer Centricity*.[7] As anyone in the customer service industries will tell you, the explosive developments in technology have empowered customers around the world. Ernst and Young noted that by 2020, there will be more than 50 billion smartphones connected to the internet around the world, and those mobile devices will be the main way most people will connect with the internet. This has massive implications for CEOs in terms of how they will manage future crises, and in terms of the expectations of immediacy consumers will have when something goes wrong. The report concluded that customers are increasingly more hedonistic ("It's all about me"), more demanding, and more sophisticated.

That space between what those increasingly sophisticated customers think of your brand, and what you want your brand to be, was the topic of a powerful 2013 study by the international PR firm Fleishman-Hillard called the *Authenticity Gap*.[8] It analyzed 20 industry sectors in the United States, Germany, and China to determine which categories are best meeting consumer expectations. The goal was to give CEOs a better road map to more authentic interactions with customers. "We looked across the industry and saw a lot of different reputation studies out there, but none was giving the C-suite very actionable insights into what they could do to change their reputation in the minds of various stakeholders," said FleishmanHillard's Marjorie Benzkofer.[9] What they found was that a major driver of how consumers feel about a company is how they observe the behaviors of senior management. It's a telling sign for CEOs that the study showed that attributes related to corporate behavior were as important to those surveyed as attributes associated with actual customer care.

What all of this adds up to is that the era of hiding a CEO under a bushel basket is long gone. Consumers not only want to know who the CEO is, but they want to form an opinion about him or her—an opinion that will feed into their view of the brand. That is why Chip Wilson could no longer lead Lululemon as CEO after his unfortunate comments in a TV interview about problems with company's yoga pants being caused by the shape of women's bodies. He became far too toxic to be attached to Lululemon's brand.

Increasingly we will see CEOs getting out proactively on crisis management, as Target CEO Gregg Steinhafel did when he sent an email to his customers apologizing for the 2013 credit card breach and updating them on where the issue stood. Is it surprising then that the "Best Perceived Brand" in 2013 according to more than 1.2 million interviews conducted by YouGov Brand Index was Amazon? Here is a company whose CEO, Jeff Bezos, is one of the most well-known CEOs in the world, and who, according to the people who conducted the survey, benefited from "an insane focus on the customer."

40 – 50% of a consumer's perception of any given brand is formed by what they know about the CEO or the management of that company.

Most of the academic research now shows that about 40 to 50 percent of a consumer's perception of any given brand is formed by what they know about the CEO or the management of that company. Bezos is a big part of why consumers hold Amazon in such high regard. For many years, that was also the case with Bill Gates at Microsoft and Facebook's Mark Zuckerberg. The CEO as the brand is the way we are headed now. As we speed toward a 50-billion mobile devices world, there is no turning back.

## Notes

1. http://en.wikipedia.org/wiki/There_are_known_knowns
2. www.brandfog.com/CEOSocialMediaSurvey/BRANDfog_2014_CEO_Survey.pdf
3. http://blog.hubspot.com/marketing/ceos-you-cant-afford-to-ignore-social-media-anymore
4. www.ceo.com/social-ceo-report-2013/
5. www.webershandwick.com/uploads/news/files/Social-CEO-Study.pdf
6. http://fastlane.gm.com/2014/03/26/mary-barra-answers-ignition-switch-recall-questions/
7. www.ey.com/Publication/vwLUAssets/The_journey_toward_greater_customer_centricity_-_US/$FILE/Customer_Centricity_Paper_29_April_Final_US.pdf
8. http://fleishmanhillard.com/2013/04/news-and-opinions/mind-the-gap-new-fleishman-hillard-research-shows-an-authenticity-gap-for-companies-across-the-globe/
9. http://fleishmanhillard.com/profile/marjorie-benzkofer/

# Chapter 7

# Social Media Matters

MANY OF US have security systems in our homes or condos. We have alarm systems in our cars that set the horns honking and sirens beeping. Many seniors who live independently wear a medical alert button on a necklace or bracelet so that they can warn health professionals or family members of an immediate health emergency. We go to the doctor for our annual physical to make sure our bodies' systems are functioning well and we are not facing a pending health crisis caused, for example, by high blood pressure.

We are surrounded in our daily lives by these early warning systems. Some automobiles now have detector systems that cause a red flashing light and repeated beeping if someone or something is approaching too closely on the left, right, from ahead, or from behind. This feature is expected to be standard in a few years. Some of these cars will actually pre-load the braking system when the front detector goes off, anticipating you jamming your foot on the brake even before it gets there. Mercedes has a system that causes the steering wheel to vibrate as a warning if you drift out of your lane—one step closer to the self-driving cars Google has been testing.

It would be unthinkable to live without these early warning systems; most would consider it reckless. And that is why we should never consider foregoing social media monitoring. Social media is your alarm system. Social media is your early warning radar of an impending potential disaster.

We live in an era where marketing is being turned on its head because the way consumer content has turned upside down. When I grew up you were forced to choose between ABC, NBC, or CBS. That was basically it. If you wanted to watch cartoons as a kid, you got up on Saturday morning—you looked forward to Saturday mornings because the cartoons were on! As for the news, Walter Cronkite was . . . he was *Walter Cronkite*! He delivered the news! He told us that Kennedy had been shot.

Advertisers could buy saturation in any given market fairly easily. Channels were fewer. Brands were defined by what the brand marketers told us. Coca-Cola, for example, was The Real Thing. McDonald's told us: "You deserve a break today!" Chevrolet was "The Heartbeat of America." Everybody knew that Kentucky Fried Chicken was "Finger-lickin' good!" That pink bunny from Energizer? It just kept "going and going and going." If you used the Yellow Pages, you could "let your fingers do the walking."

Today, it is the opposite. There are fewer universally known jingles and brand slogans. Instead, consumers define the fast food chains, car companies, soft drinks, and retail stores. Giant corporations like McDonald's have been forced to react. There can never be another Walter Cronkite because we live in a several-hundred-channel universe, complete with 24/7 news and weather channels and instant access to online news sites.

Not to mention that TV broadcast advertising—still not entirely irrelevant—is increasingly undermined by the fast-forward button on personal video recorders (PVRs). For those under 30, broadcast TV itself is being undermined by the increasing popularity of simply cutting the cable off and relying on internet downloads of commercial-free programs.

At the end of 2013, Tom Rutledge, CEO of cable TV–giant Charter Communications, told Wall Street analysts that he "was surprised" to learn that 1.3 million of his company's 5.5 million customers only want broadband internet. As for cable TV, those 1.3 million said "no thanks." It's a universe where the influence (and income) of the large TV networks is waning and unless they find another way, will be replaced by streaming video-on-demand sites like Netflix (which has already produced its own drama series including the critically acclaimed *House of Cards* and *Orange is the New Black*), iTunes, Amazon, and other on-demand broadcast sites that will only proliferate in the years ahead. Those who've cut the cable are connecting to their TV monitors instead with Apple TV, Roku, and Google's Chromecast, to name a few.

Forget about needing to tell your teenagers to turn off the TV and do their homework, because they don't watch TV. They need to be told to log off social media sites and instant messaging platforms and do their homework.

## Customers Define the Brand

In short, it's an era where you no longer define your brand. Your customers define your brand. Your brand is what people say about you. Amazon's Jeff Bezos famously explained it as: "Your brand is what people say about you when you are not in the room." Your brand is thousands of interactions where customers' expectations are pitted against the actual experience they have with your company. If your company promotes its outstanding customer service, for example, people will judge it by the expectation they have. Was that person helpful on the phone? Was the delivery made on time? If I can't make this work, can I get help? Will they have it in stock? Will it get delivered on time?

And there it is again: public expectations; ingrained perceptions. When you exceed expectations you win. When you shatter negative perception, you win. It's when you fail to live up to expectations and reinforce negative perceptions (your actions further entrench them) that you lose. But one thing you can be sure of is that the alarm will sound first on social media.

The room you are not in, to extend Bezos' analogy, is called social media and that is where people are talking about you. So set up your monitoring with a reputable service, make sure you have selected the proper relevant key search words and make sure your team has identified influential individuals or online communities that relate to your business or organization. The reason that early warning is so essential is this: You will need every minute of advance warning you can possibly get because of the blazing speed at which today's crises travel. As if managing a crisis isn't difficult or stressful enough, consider that more than one-in-four major crises (28 percent) will spread internationally within 60 minutes on social media. That was the finding published in 2013 by the Holmes Report based on research conducted by the international law firm Freshfields Bruckhaus Deringer. Wait 24 hours and more than two-thirds of crises (69 percent) have spread internationally.[1]

## Social Media Can Create the Crisis

In addition to this astonishing speed, remember that social media channels are not just a vehicle to spread the flash fire to exponentially larger audiences by the minute; these channels are often where the crisis originates. Many social media-based crises are self-inflicted by a famous athlete or entertainer, or by a politician, or well-known business leader. If your social media gaffe is egregious enough, you don't even need to be well known.

One of the most stunning examples of how fast a crisis travels on social media is the case of Justine Sacco, the former Director of Communications for U.S. media giant IAC. Immediately prior to boarding a flight to South Africa in late 2013, she tweeted: "Going to Africa. Hope I don't get AIDS. Just kidding! I'm white." In any context, it was a horrible, horrible decision. Think of it this way, if you wouldn't say it live on air during an international broadcast being watched by hundred of millions of people, then you shouldn't tweet it or post it to Facebook (which is essentially the same broadcast through a different medium), no matter how clever, or ironic, you believe your post to be. Sacco posted her tweet and then spent the next 12 hours on the flight en route to Capetown, without any internet access.

By the time she landed and booted her cellphone back up, there was a global firestorm of controversy. It was something the *New Yorker* magazine called "a ruinous flash-fame . . . (followed by) a barrage of violent misogyny, terrible in its blunt force and grim inevitability."[2] Gawker had posted her tweet, which accelerated its viral expansion across the globe. Someone online tracked down the flight details and a new hashtag, *#HasJustineLandedYet*, erupted in yet another viral wave across the worldwide web. By the time she landed, the story was being reported by news sites around the world.

She did get a chance to apologize on social media, but the truth is that the decision to fire her had probably been made before the wheels of her jet even touched down on the tarmac. As the *New Yorker* pointed out, here was evidence that you don't need to be Justin Bieber, or Brett Farve, or Anthony Weiner, or anybody famous—if your tweet is horrible enough it can destroy your reputation in an instant. It is a cautionary tale many have still failed to grasp.

It's a particularly acute problem with athletes who emerge from the college ranks into professional sports. Almost every pro sports league, including the National Football League, Major League Baseball, the National Basketball Association, and the National Hockey League, trains rookie players either on a league-wide basis or a team-by-team basis on the dangers and practices of social media. It's often about the so-called "trolls," people who surf around on places like Twitter trying to pick fights with well-known athletes or celebrities in order to set off a social media online argument, which the trolls seem to delight in as a form of validation and 15 minutes of fame.

An alarming number of social media crises involving celebrities of all sorts from politics to show business to the corporate world have been sparked by trolls. Others have been sparked by alcohol, the social media version of "drunk-dialing." But the truth is, once you press the post button that tweet lives on forever, even if you delete not just the tweet but your entire Twitter account. Some day 20 years from now when you run for office, or when you are vetted for a C-suite job or Board of Directors posting, it will turn up to haunt you. So beware!

## Social Media Is Just Another Channel

This is why using social media to respond to a crisis in your organization is not just about speed, but about getting it right. Think of social media as just another media channel. It's no different than a TV or radio interview. It is just being broadcast in a digital format. But it is being broadcast. News increasingly breaks on social media. The Pew Research Journalism Project reported in Fall 2013 that roughly half of all Twitter and Facebook users get their news from their social media feeds on those sites. Twitter, in particular, is a fascinating real-time qualitative research sample (depending on who you follow) on any breaking news or major event. And the use of hashtags allow you to customize your own broadcast.

A few years ago I was among a group of people working to help Jim Balsillie, the co-founder of RIM (maker of the Blackberry), in his attempt to buy the NHL's Phoenix Coyotes out of bankruptcy. On the dates when I couldn't get to Phoenix to attend the bankruptcy court, I would simply refresh the Twitter feeds of two or three reporters I knew who were sitting in the courtroom. They were tweeting literally a blow-by-blow: "Now the lawyer for the NHL has argued this . . ."; "Now Balsillie's lawyer has responded . . ."; "Now the judge seems peeved and he's commenting that . . ."—it was extraordinary. It was almost as good as TV cameras in a courtroom, except with commentary.

This is how issues play out in real time on Twitter. And it is truly stunning—and a bit addictive—to watch it happen. The day of the terrible Spring 2013 bombing of the Boston Marathon, tweets on the topic went suddenly from a few thousand that morning to more than 6 million. The *Boston Globe* used Twitter as its live feed for breaking news. Subsequently, Boston Police posted pictures on Twitter of suspects wanted in the bombing in a request for public help with the investigation.

Police everywhere regularly use social media in investigations. Press releases have become almost passé. Derek Jeter made the major announcement that 2014 would be his final MLB season not via press release, but on Facebook. Certainly for most people under age 30 in the developed world, Twitter is one of the first places they will go for breaking news, as opposed to, say, CNN.

## There's No Longer a Choice

And that is why I always counsel corporate leaders who say, "I don't want to go there, it's not right for us," that they no longer have a choice. They just don't. Anyone who would set out to ignore social media in a crisis is playing a reputational version of Russian Roulette. It's not just about losing the crisis that you didn't see coming; it's also about losing the opportunity to identify emerging issues and take action before they develop into full-blown crises. Ultimately it is about squandering the better odds of winning the crisis and enhancing your brand and the loyalty of your current and, hopefully future, customers.

So how do we do that? Any number of social media agencies or public relations agencies in your city can provide you with specific advice tailored to your company or organization. The main decisions are determined by how big you are. There are major telecommunications firms in North America that monitor Twitter and Facebook so closely that within an hour or so of a customer posting a complaint (usually *#fail*) about their product, the company has sent a tweet or Facebook message to the customer to engage them and try to solve the problem. These large companies also keep detailed statistics on the types of social media mentions they receive and look for trends—or early warning signals. Large organizations hire full-time "content managers" to monitor and engage with social media audiences.

You can also contract directly with a PR or digital agency, such as FleishmanHillard, Edelman, Weber Shandwick, or Hill+Knowlton to provide services that will pull social media monitoring reports for you daily, based on keyword searches, using systems such as Sysomos and Radian6. What's critically important is not just to "listen" to what people are saying about you in that "other room" of social media that Bezos described, but to know what to do with that information. It's data-rich in insights for your marketing department.

## Act on Social Media Reports

Beyond those benefits, there also needs to be a fast-track escalation process that feeds into your organization's crisis communications plan. As we've talked about before, ideally this will involve a series of interim steps to engage the persons or organizations involved to try to manage the issue to a resolution; but failing that there must be a way to trigger the early warning system of a full-blown crisis.

I know of organizations that did a decent job of social media monitoring, but then when a crisis hit they asked, "Why didn't our social media monitoring pick up on that?" The answer, invariably, is it did, but nobody read it, or if they read it, nobody acted on it. At times, it can seem numbingly repetitive when you are reading the same social media reports day in and day out. It takes discipline. One busy day or two of failing to review them and ignoring them becomes a habit. My advice is ignore these reports no more than you would ignore a red flashing check engine light on your dashboard.

This social media early warning system is there for a reason: to alert you. What you do with it at that point is up to you. But it's best to have redundancies built in; your PR or digital agency should flag you; or perhaps your half dozen content managers (usually young hires right out of college) should flag you. You might also request that both your Marketing department and your Corporate Communications department receive a report so that either or both will flag you. Even your in-house legal counsel could be included in the distribution list. The important point is that the early warning system should only fail when multiple response systems fail. And if that happens, it will be time to re-evaluate how you monitor.

Then it becomes about the response you deliver via social media. It needs to be authentic. Nothing will backfire faster and have you "flamed" with posts criticizing you than a cheesy-sounding post filled with PR spin. It's always best to engage directly with some of the people who are your biggest critics on Twitter. You won't necessarily win them over, but you will demonstrate to the social media community that you are "real" and that your responses are authentic.

Consider the case of Lieutenant General David Morrison, head of the Australian Army. "If that does not suit you, then *get out.*" With those words, spoken bluntly and viewed by almost 1.5 million people around the world on YouTube, a new bar was set for crisis communications management via social media.

Morrison was responding to a summer 2013 *Sydney Morning Herald* story (June 14, 2013) about an "internet sex ring" which allegedly involved members of the Army sharing nude photos or videos of women—some of them members of the same Army—as a challenge to other members of the ring to attempt to have sex with the same women. It was alleged that in some cases, some of the women filmed in shared videos were not aware they were being videotaped. Most of the emails containing the videos and images were allegedly sent using the Australian Defence Force's email system.

Morrison demonstrated a barely-controlled rage in his response on YouTube. No one could have accused him of not being authentic, nor being tone deaf to the severity of the topic. "The same goes for those who think that toughness is built on humiliating others," he stated. "Every one of us is responsible for the culture and reputation of our Army and the environment in which we work. If you become aware of any individual degrading another, then show moral courage and take a stand against it. No one has ever explained to me how the exploitation or degradation of others enhances capability or honors the traditions of the Australian Army. I will be *ruthless* in ridding the Army of anyone who cannot live up to its values." Morrison also set up a Defence Abuse Response Taskforce, designed to allow any others who may have been impacted by such abuse to step forward and report it.

The reality, in this case, is that no amount of social media monitoring would have provided an early warning of this crisis. Often that is just the nature of a crisis—it is sudden, it is explosive, and it requires an immediate and forceful response. What made Morrison's response so effective was the palpable anger he demonstrated on a YouTube video.[3] Effective responses to catastrophic crises require a combination of logic and emotion; people equally need to see that your organization is acting on the issue, as well as they need to feel your emotional reaction to it. If the crisis angers people, chances are you should be angered as the leader of that organization, and remorseful. If the crisis strikes people as particularly sad and tragic, your response needs to be reflective of that reality. If viewers had felt that Morrison was reluctantly making the video, or that he was dispassionate about the issue, it could easily have backfired.

An insincere apology just fans the flames. In this case, an insincere apology or a refusal to discuss aspects of the event could have fed into the public's preconceived notions that military leaders tend to be secretive and cover up for other members of the military. Instead, Morrison shattered that perception, somewhat surprisingly, and lashed out at members of his Army over the allegations. He was widely praised.

## Authenticity Matters

Your response has to be the real deal because now, more than ever, the public is aware of, and extremely skeptical about, the so-called "PR spin doctors" who issue statements of apology and send their clients to rehab. It reeks of self-serving glibness. Enter as evidence, that very same summer of the powerful Morrison video, the Paula Deen fiasco. The so-called Queen of Southern cooking made an apology—three actually—after she was forced to admit she had used a racial slur (the N-word) in the past when speaking to her employees. Deen was fired from her Food Network show and dropped by sponsors because of the fumbling, insincere, and self-centered approach she took to apologizing.

Her first apology blamed her age and where she was raised, noting in a statement that she was ". . . born 60 years ago when America's South had schools that were segregated, different bathrooms, different restaurants, and Americans rode in different parts of the bus. . . ." That was Fail #1.

Her second apology went out on a 45-second video[4] in which she appears confused about what she is saying, with several long pauses and unexplained blank stares into the camera. It caused even further damage. By now, Deen's reputation was in free-fall.

A third video attempt at an apology went terribly wrong. Deen cast herself as the victim in this video, after standing up Matt Lauer on the *Today Show* because "I was physically not able (to do it) this morning. The pain has been tremendous that I have caused to myself and to others," she stated. She went on to complain that she and her family "aren't the kind of people the press is wanting to say we are."

Then, the woman who had failed at two former attempts at apologies, went even further down the road of self-interest, as opposed to public interest. She talked about having worked 24 years to build her business, having worked at times "too hard." Many observers were offended that it appeared she was trying to turn herself into the victim.

That fully played out a week later when she finally found the strength to talk to Lauer on the *Today Show* and warned people who themselves had done things they regretted that they shouldn't throw stones—presumably at her. In tears, Deen said that those who had never done anything they regretted could "please pick up that stone and throw it so hard at my head that it kills me. Please. I want to meet you. I want to meet you. I is what I is (*sic*) and I'm not changing."

At that point Deen was beyond repair in terms of her personal brand. It left few options other than to just go away for a while and leave the public arena. She has since started to rebuild, but some of her behavior has remained unchanged. As CNN reported[5] in early 2014: *"Paula Deen feels like 'that black,' gay football player."* She had done an interview with *People* magazine about her comeback in which she'd said: "I feel like [the words] 'embattled' or 'disgraced' will always follow my name. . . . It's like that black football player who recently came out," she said, referring to Michael Sam, who starred for the University of Missouri. "He said, 'I just want to be known as a football player. I don't want to be known as a gay football player.' I know exactly what he's saying." So even as part of her comeback, Deen is apparently still portraying herself as the victim.

In these two approaches—Morrison's and Deen's—you can see the difference between taking a self-interested approach versus a public interest-focused approach. Morrison's self-interest would have been to defend the Army. Instead, Morrison put the public interest first and called out those who allegedly participated. Then he put in place a program to bring any further degradation to light. Deen, on the other hand, failed the sincerity test and then went into self-pity mode, leaning heavily on her own self-interest as a crutch.

So if there is a lesson here it is this: There is no mystery about social media. It's the same approach, the same steps, that must be taken in a crisis situation. It's just a conversation on a much more massive, online scale.

## Notes

1. www.holmesreport.com/expertknowledge-info/14300/Social-Media-Requires-Faster-Crisis-Response-Survey-Says.aspx

2. www.newyorker.com/online/blogs/books/2014/01/first-thought-worst-thought.html?utm_source=tny&utm_medium=email&utm_campaign=dailyemail&mbid=nl_Daily%20%2898%29

3. www.youtube.com/watch?v=QaqpoeVgr8U#t=31

4. Slate.com, June 21, 2013

5. www.cnn.com/2014/02/27/showbiz/celebrity-news-gossip/paula-deen-comeback/

# Chapter 8

# Monday Morning Armchair Quarterbacks

WHAT MANY CEOs and senior leaders find infuriating in today's crisis climate is the second-guessing and criticism that comes from so-called Monday Morning Armchair Quarterbacks. We're not talking about debates as to whether the Broncos should have punted instead of going for it on fourth down. But it's the same syndrome. "Why didn't they warn us in the past that they'd had contamination issues with this product and it could make people sick?" "Why can't they tell us when our flight will take off? Are they not prepared for winter weather?"

There are endless could-haves, would-haves, and should-haves. Who doesn't enjoy a good round of armchair quarterbacking? Very few people these days, it seems. Isn't that what coworkers often do when they go together to the bar for an after-work beer? Who hasn't lost a campaign or failed to meet a project's goals and wondered, "If we'd just implemented that idea, at that critical time, things might have turned out differently." Even when we get into a heated argument with someone, we often later think of the things we could have said, or should have said.

In fact, we've become a society of second-guessers. Try it yourself: The next time a crisis breaks across mainstream news channels do a hashtag search for it on Twitter and read some of the posts people have put up. You will find that 9-in-10 posts are snarky criticisms aimed at what the organization at the center of the crisis should have done. In fact a Pew Research study (March 5, 2013) confirmed that Twitter brings out the meanness in people, and in fact is more darkly negative than the overall population when measured against public opinion surveys.

Ditto Facebook. Just look at the Facebook page of any well-known brand and you will see all of the posts by second-guessers and naysayers—as I write this the first 25 public posts (and they continued) on the American Airlines Facebook page were all negative. Both Twitter and Facebook debates are often populated with people uninformed about the facts of any given matter, but that doesn't stop them from stating their opinions on random topics.

As it should be—that is just the online democracy that we live in. But make no mistake, there are a plethora of so-called "haters" in social media who seem to thrive on the negativity. Twitter, in particular, is filled with them. It has become fashionable on some controversial issues to set up new fake Twitter identities simply to mock a person or an idea. The cauldron of negativity has brewed such a nasty stew that even the most mild-mannered participants are quitting the habit.

Stewart Cink is one of the most gentlemanly players on the PGA Tour. He was also one of the early adopters of Twitter and a real social media leader among golf's elite players. And yet, on February 2014 he told Golf.com: "Over Twitter's life, it seems like the negativity has gotten out of control. So for someone who reads all their replies, it just gets depressing. People get a kick out of being negative. They don't expect anybody to read it. Well, I read my replies. And it got to be pretty annoying." Twitter's golf commentators—and I use that term loosely, because we're not talking about Johnny Miller here—called Cink names like *#worstmajorwinner ever*. And then there was a small firestorm of sarcasm when Cink, who is bald, took his golf hat off to shake hands with a playing partner at the 2014 Sony Open, and the photo of his tan line became a Twitter punch line.

It demonstrates that people on Twitter will spew hatred at anyone, even people like Cink who've never done anything to offend. They are equal opportunity haters. Even feel good initiatives are fair game, such as the New York Police Department public relations request that people tweet pictures of themselves with NYPD officers—which was then flamed and became an international news story and PR black eye when the NYPD's Twitter feed was filled with negative posts and pictures, some of which alleged police brutality.

Sadly, it often seems as if what drives these Twitter threads is one-upmanship over who can be the most clever critic or post the funniest cutting pun. To many experienced observers of social media, this is when established platforms (remember MySpace?) begin to wane and fall out of favor, only to be replaced by something new and shiny. Time will tell.

## Don't Write Off Negativity

So in a crisis situation, does that mean we can write off most of the negativity on social media? The short answer is no. The key question for any organization or company to ask itself during a crisis is who are these nattering nabobs of negativity (as William Safire famously wrote for Spiro Agnew)? Who do they represent? After all, two organizations at odds over a major public policy issue could be waging a donnybrook on Twitter that one would think represented a deeply divided public—only to discover it was about a dozen avid tweeters on each side of the issue having at each other, while millions of people in the community paid absolutely no—or very little—attention.

There are times when Twitter or Facebook represent special interests and isolated views. There are times when the people tweeting are either crazy or just spewing nonsense. But there are also times—the Los Angeles Clippers' owner Donald Sterling racism scandal for example—when the social media feeding frenzy cuts across all demographic lines and includes people who don't come at the issue from a special-interest perspective.

This is where your social media monitoring requires some deeper investigation. Twitter volume, as we saw in the Sterling case or with the Tiger Woods scandal for example, is a key indicator. We've also talked about the need to identify influencers on social media, those with large followings or who get re-tweeted or replied to often.

Some people on Twitter identify themselves and who they represent

—I do. Most journalists do. If you see a reporter for the daily newspaper in your city post a tweet about a topic, you can expect to see a story about it in the newspaper the next day. Similarly, if you see a journalist respond to a tweet and engage with someone on Twitter, a story will likely follow. Twitter and Facebook have become rich resources for story ideas and citizen feedback for journalists—and much of the survival of mainstream journalism relies on its ability to effectively integrate and participate in social media communities.

You can also go more deeply beyond the surface of someone's tweet to see what they have posted about before. Their tweets will tell the story of someone who uses Twitter for a specific purpose, or to drive a specific agenda. Perhaps they re-tweet or favorite every tweet they see about a sustainable environmental initiative. Many of their tweets are criticisms of major energy corporations. If you are one of those energy companies and you find yourself on the receiving end of a nasty tweet from this person, you can understand where they are coming from and acknowledge that they are likely part of a group of stakeholders opposed to what your company does and therefore not likely to be influenced by outreach from your organization. However, if you examine more closely the tweet of a woman who replied to that tweet and added her own criticism, only to find that she is bank branch employee and mother of three kids who normally tweets about soccer and Little League games, that might indicate a broader, more mainstream concern with your company's policies and something that should be of much greater concern to you, if it continues to happen.

This is the early warning alarm we have talked about earlier. When you begin to see certain sentiments from Twitter users who could be best described as being part of the general population—the so-called genpop—that is often a signal that public opinion is shifting. The hard-core Twitter radicals will always try to shift public opinion, but the vast majority of people are fair minded and use common sense. They recognize the hyperbole and craziness for what it is.

So when you are in the middle of a crisis, it is best not to rely on social media as the sole measure of public opinion on any given issue. Test it against more statistically reliable public opinion research, or at least compare it to your call center volumes, for instance, or to something qualitative by reaching out to a group of influencers and stakeholders to get their take on the situation. You may even decide you need to do a focus group to look more closely at perceptions about your issue.

## Time Travel

A big part of the second-guessing that immediately occurs during a crisis has to do with what I call time travel. By that I mean, media and the public—those so-called "citizen reporters" on Twitter and Facebook—will second-guess your company, its motives, your intentions, your intelligence, and your truthfulness by discussing things you did or didn't do in the past, or things you will or will not do in the future.

Time travel back into the past happens, just as it does in a media interview, when your critics argue that you should have done $X$ in the past and then today's outcome would be different. If you had better quality control measures in place, your product would not have harmed so many people, for example. The other direction is into the future, as in, "If this continues they'll be out of business in six months—I'm selling my shares today." Or: "If these incompetent idiots cannot find the source of this spill, more people will die."

Remember the public interest in all of this and try to resist the temptation to take personal offense because that would be you putting your own self-interest first. Remember that social media is just an inherently negative place. And then move forward to address these concerns, where legitimate, in an authentic and factual way, with both the mainstream media and on social media.

> Social media is just an inherently negative place.

The most important element here is to avoid time travel. When NBA Commissioner Adam Silver held a press conference to announce the lifetime ban on Donald Sterling and his intention to get the required

75 percent of owners to agree to force Sterling to sell the Los Angeles Clippers, he did not time travel into the future. He could have. Silver was asked what would happen if he failed to get the required 75 percent of owners on board with his plan. He declined to speculate on that, saying that he was confident the owners would back his plan. Similarly, Silver avoided time travel in reverse. He was asked several times if he could have avoided the embarrassment to the NBA if he and other league officials had paid more attention to Sterling's alleged racist comments in the past. Again, Silver professionally declined to entertain that time travel and stayed focused on the here-and-now facts in a textbook display of how to manage in a crisis.

It is absolutely critical in a crisis to maintain your focus on the here-and-now facts—today, as you know them to be. It is fine to answer "I don't know," when pressed on certain facts if you do not have the answer, so long as you are clear about the process underway to gather those facts and the timeline in which you plan to share them publicly. Do not pretend to know more than you actually do know.

> It is fine to answer "I don't know," when pressed on certain facts if you do not have the answer. Do not pretend to know more than you actually do know.

It will require great discipline on your part, but let the second-guessers guess. Do not speculate if you don't know the answer in terms of future developments. Don't speculate about whether you wished certain things were done differently in the past. Just deal with the facts, in the moment. You need the information you share with the public to be absolutely factual and accurate. Nothing will damage your credibility more, or derail your attempts to effectively manage a crisis, than to state as fact something that isn't true, is mistaken, or is less than the full and clear picture. Your iron-clad commitment is to find out what went wrong and fix it so it won't happen again.

Of course it is impossible to have a discussion about Monday Morning Armchair Quarterbacks in crisis communications without talking about the mainstream media. Full disclosure: I wrote for Canada's largest newspaper on a daily basis for 22 years—the last 17 in satellite bureaus where I worked with colleagues from TV, radio, magazines, and other newspapers. That entitles me, arguably, to submit that I understand how the media works and why they do what they do. And for the most part, I staunchly defend the work journalists do and their right to do it.

I have always been a firm believer in that old Mark Twain quote: "Never pick a fight with people who buy ink by the barrel." Having said that, I will not, and have not, ever hesitated to deal forcefully—up to and including through legal means—with journalists or media outlets who treat my clients in an unprofessional or unfair way. I advise you to do the same.

But I would also advise you of this: Over more than three decades I can tell you that in about 95 percent of the cases I have witnessed when an individual, company, or organization complained about unfair treatment at the hands of the media, the media in question were just doing their job. That is the reality. Just like the reality of the court of public opinion. You can debate it, argue it, fight about and turn it inside out, but it is a true fact. And the worst offenders in terms of self-pitying attacks on so-called unfair journalism are the people like Paula Deen who are completely engrossed in their own self-interest and have lost sight of the public interest.

The media never lose sight of the public interest; the role of journalists is largely to defend the public interest against more powerful individuals and institutions they perceive to be acting purely out of self-interest. Most people in the PR business have lost count of the number of times they've heard a CEO or a VP communications say to them: "Hey, the press is killing us. Make it stop." That's self-interest. It ignores the issue of why the media are on the attack. Trust me, if they weren't selling newspapers, getting eyeballs on their broadcasts, or hits on their website, they wouldn't continue. So the public must have an interest in what they're reporting.

I can remember a particularly embattled politician I covered as a reporter who was lambasted by attacks and innuendo day in and day out for months. At times, as the newly elected politician that he was, he fed these stories by saying silly things in media scrums, or by not being prepared. Sadly, he has since passed away. But he was a lovely man. Everyone liked him. Even the reporters who skewered him liked him, privately. It was just business.

One day, he asked me if I would go for lunch with him to talk about his situation. He complained about how he was being treated by the media—no differently than the complaints commonly heard by PR people every day. I said to him, "You are in charge of all transportation right? That is your portfolio right?" "Yes," he said. "What do you care about? What bothers you that you'd like to fix?" He said what really upset him was the recent spate of flying transport truck tires, deadly giant steel and rubber projectiles that were increasingly flying off trucks (due to loose or rusted bolts that hadn't been inspected) going full speed on area highways. One had recently crashed through a woman's windshield and killed her.

Pretty quickly he understood where our conversation was headed. My advice was to champion truck safety and highway safety. Be out there every single day, if he could be, driving home that message and getting things done to make the highways safer. I didn't realize at the time that I was basically telling him to set aside his own self-interest and focus on the public interest. And I remember, in the months that followed, being a bit surprised by how often I turned on the 6 P.M. news and there he was, standing beside some busy highway, doing media interviews talking about his latest efforts to tackle the problem. His communications team did a great job. In very short order, he felt like reporters were treating him fairly and indeed they were, because his focus on this issue in terms of the public interest aligned with theirs. He gave them stories that their public audiences cared about and they happily reported them as news. It worked the way the relationship is supposed to work.

## Winners and Losers

The Monday Morning Armchair Quarterback syndrome doesn't just apply to those who will inevitably second-guess how you handle a crisis, or how you ended up being embroiled in a crisis. It extends to how you communicated—or didn't communicate—about it. It extends to how effectively, or terribly, you conducted media interviews.

There is a much greater appetite than ever before among the general public for discussion about how well someone does in a media interview. It still surprises me, quite frankly, that PR people like me get asked to come on TV or talk radio, or to be interviewed by a newspaper, to talk about how successfully or unsuccessfully someone in the spotlight handled their interactions with reporters. "Well, he was doing okay until this moment right here, where he parroted the negative." Who cares, other than the principals? We all do, apparently.

It has become a bit of a sport, the kind where we pick winners and losers. Mass media, primarily TV and movie dramas, regularly peel back the veil on media interactions and show the public the strategic considerations and tactical tools that are fed into the preparation for a major media interview, including media training depicted on such TV shows as *The Good Wife*.

A seminal moment in modern times, in this regard, was the 1992 interview[1] Bill and Hillary Clinton appeared in, together, with Steve Kroft of *60 Minutes*. Bill Clinton, then Governor of Arkansas, had just been anointed the Democratic frontrunner for the party's presidential nomination, by *TIME* magazine no less. But six days after the *TIME* cover story, the mainstream media widely reported a tabloid story alleging Clinton had carried on a 12-year extra-marital affair with a former TV reporter named Gennifer Flowers.

Bill Clinton's character had quickly become the central issue that threatened to derail his presidential dream before it had barely begun; it was the equivalent of a political crisis communications earthquake. Kroft quoted Clinton, saying that the would-be Democratic nominee had "been saying all week you need to put this issue behind you." Kroft then gave Clinton the opportunity to say that he'd never had any extra-marital affairs. "I have acknowledged wrongdoing. I have acknowledged causing pain in my marriage," Clinton replied. And with that, he was back in the race. The trials about his character and alleged womanizing continued, but Clinton soldiered on.

This interview was fascinating in that it sparked the first real discussion and debate about how subjects prepare for these kinds of interviews, whether the interview "worked" or not, and even the minute details, such as the headband Hillary wore. It has become standard practice today for embattled public figures to begin the reputational rehabilitation process by doing a major TV interview: on *60 Minutes,* with Oprah Winfrey, or perhaps Ellen DeGeneres. Public cynicism (and Twitter negativity) has even extended to the standard celebrity scandal process of press conference or major interview, followed by absence from the public stage while attending a rehab program of some sort, followed by the dramatic re-emergence and comeback story.

> It has become standard practice today for embattled public figures to begin the reputational rehabilitation process by doing a major TV interview.

There are no more secrets about how these crises are handled, but rather there is an ongoing sort of color commentary about how well each stage of the process was handled. Nothing is worse than beginning the process with a press conference or video intended to serve as a "coming clean" moment that backfires, as it did for Southern chef Paula Deen in three separate attempts.

Tiger Woods famously did it at a press conference during which he took no questions and then disappeared into a rehab program, to never speak publicly about those issues again. As much coverage as there was of the Woods scandal, the coverage assessing his believability and performance at the press conference was just as voluminous.

Think about New Jersey Governor Chris Christie and the bridge scandal. The coverage of what Christie said, how he said it, the techniques he used, and how believable he was at his first press conference was almost as heavy as coverage about breaking news elements in the story. It has become nearly a test now that the public and media want that person or company to pass. Can they handle the hot lights? Can they answer? Clinton passed the test in 1992 with that *60 Minutes* interview and proved that a skilled communicator can step up and survive, then thrive.

So if you are the main spokesperson for your company or organization when a crisis hits, or you work closely with that person, understand in advance that what will count as much as what you say in that seminal communications moment is how you say it. Fairly or unfairly, if you say it badly, or you trip up on some of the more common media interview traps, your shaky performance could easily overshadow the content of your message.

## Media Training

While you hear in any crisis communications discussion information about protocols and planning, running drills, and even pre-drafting press releases that cover the most likely crises your organization may face, don't overlook good old fashioned media training. There just is no substitute. Media training is a skill set that you don't just acquire in one sitting, either. I don't think any C-suite executive or organizational spokesperson should ever do an interview without being media-trained and developing their skills on an ongoing basis—period.

You need to level the playing field. Reporters are skilled at what they do. They do it every single day. They've conducted thousands of interviews and there isn't a situation or a direction an interview can take that will surprise them. They are also a little bit like sharks. Like sensing blood in the water, they can smell when an interview subject is willing to go places they shouldn't be, so they will happily take them further and further down that road.

Having said that, reporters are not inherently evil. What they want is a great story, preferably an exclusive. What they want is to meet their deadline. They need you to get right to the point, and they need you not to waste their time chasing down information you could have easily provided to them. Too many communicators, in my view, still view the media as a necessary evil. They are just folks who are trying to get the job done and survive in a business (journalism) whose model is broken and whose profitability is plunging. These are uncertain times for people in media. But they are professionals.

Just like lawyers or doctors or accountants, there are great journalists and there are solid, reliable journalists. And like those other professionals, even a few dodgy practitioners. But for the most part, unprofessional or under-achieving reporters do not survive in today's media climate. If you approach your interactions with them in a professional manner, you can expect they will also behave professionally.

My advice is to treat the media the same way you treat other stake-holders. Build relationships and credibility with them on an ongoing basis. Take the time to build some individual relationships with key reporters and get to know them away from the microphone.

Treat the media the same way you treat other stakeholders.

Typically what they want is access to you and your expertise, along with timely information. Reporters like to build their contact lists, too. Many of them understand that they will benefit more from a solid, long-term relationship with you than they will from burning you just for one headline. But if you expect them to understand the stresses and demands of your position, take the time to understand the stresses and demands of theirs. Take them for breakfast or lunch when you aren't asking them for something. Don't just contact them when you are pitching a story. Send them a note of congratulations when you read, or see or hear a good story they've done; again not when you need something from them, but just as an honest gesture of support for their good work.

An easy way to do that is through social media, where you can follow a reporter and re-tweet or comment on favorite stories they have done. The more you can come to an understanding of the work reporters do, the better job you will do serving their needs. That will, in turn, result in journalists doing a better job of representing the work you and your organization do.

## Keep Up Your Media Contacts

There is a video *AdAge* posted on YouTube in 2009 that I still show people today when we are discussing these issues. It's an address by Ray Kerins, then of Pfizer, discussing the approach to media relations he found at the drug manufacturer when he arrived there to lead corporate communications. He told a New York communications conference that the policy was to ignore any reporter's first call, on any topic, and only begin to respond to media requests when the second call came. "If we're not willing to engage, we only have ourselves to blame," Kerins said. "I blame myself and those of us in the industry for the bad reputation the pharmaceutical industry has. We develop life-saving medicines, that you take, that will prolong your life, that will help cure certain diseases, that will help you live a longer and healthier life. How in the hell do we have such a bad reputation? It makes no sense."

That's why Kerins put in place a new strategy during his first 20 months at Pfizer designed around two ideas, to engage and to educate reporters. He set up a program to regularly host key reporters for lunch at the company's headquarters, not to pitch a story, but just to explain to them the sorts of projects Pfizer was working on. They saw 115 reporters the first year of the program. When Kerins arrived at Pfizer, he found his new communications team was spending, on average, 15 percent of their time actually interacting with journalists. So he changed the goals of the individual communications staff members to require them to spend 50 percent of their time interacting with reporters—a threshold that was written into their job descriptions and that would be one of the key measurements in terms of calculating their compensation and bonuses.

Kerins, who was subsequently recruited to head communications for

Bayer, captured precisely the kind of approach to building relationships with the media that I advocate. And it puts the lie to any suggestion people may make that the only thing you can do to prepare for an eventual crisis is to run some crisis training sessions and simulations every few years or so, then sit back and wait. It's just not true.

Building stronger and more functional media relationships will serve you well personally throughout your career in terms of how you understand how the media works and what reporters consider newsworthy. It will also impact how your organization will be treated and perceived when the crisis strikes. It's much easier for individual reporters to attack you if they don't know you personally and they don't really understand what it is your organization does and what its policies are.

The same goes for the work you can do to foster stronger stakeholder relationships. All of these efforts are prudent, low-risk investments that will pay dividends for your organization on an ongoing basis, but they will really pay off in a crisis communications environment. When the crisis arrives it is too late to get media-trained in depth; Too late to form meaningful stakeholder or media relationships. These relationships will also help reduce the extent to which you are plagued by those pesky Monday Morning Armchair Quarterbacks.

*Note*

1.   www.cbsnews.com/news/hillarys-first-joint-interview-next-to-bill-in-92/

# Chapter 9

# The Slippery Slope of Compromise

THERE ARE TWO KINDS of slippery slopes that you don't want to find yourself on during a crisis. One is the media interview, as we have discussed, whereby you find yourself being led down a certain path by a line of questioning that leads nowhere positive. You can deal with that by taking some media training and understanding the strategic objectives behind any particular interview. But even a bad media interview can be overcome. The second kind of slippery slope is one that many organizations never recover from, the kind that causes long-term permanent damage and can mean the difference between success or failure in crisis communications management.

That is the slippery slope of compromise. If you've never managed a crisis you probably don't fully appreciate how easy it is to end up on this slope. Organizations are biased toward themselves, naturally, just as companies are biased against their competitors. You may think you are coming clean with the public about the specifics of the crisis, but the information you are sharing may be limited to some degree, it may be colored or nuanced, and important facts may be buried behind mounds of detail. All of these things represent a compromise of truthfulness. It amounts to a compromise in honesty, because consciously or unconsciously you are "spinning" or shaping the way you release the information for the benefit of your organization. There it is again, another act in the self-interest rather than the public interest.

Slipping down the slope of compromise doesn't necessarily mean you are evil or dishonest. As we discussed earlier with the fight or flight response, there is a natural tendency to flinch, to be defensive, and that manifests itself in how the facts about your crisis are collected, compiled, and released. As we covered in Chapter 6, it may also be true that this defensiveness is a cultural issue imbued throughout the organization by your CEO, who has made it clear that he or she wants to respond to the crisis but also wants to defend the company at any cost.

That's why one of the world's leading experts on business ethics argues that leaders must create an environment where these kinds of compromises are not encouraged or warmly welcomed. Professor Max Bazerman, who has served as the Straus Professor at Harvard Business School, has written, co-authored, or co-edited 18 books and more than 200 research articles in this area. He argues that leaders can shape discussion in their organizations, highlight the dangers of compromise, and ensure that all good ideas are heard—but they can only do that by "creating an environment where respect is defined as listening to and considering the ideas of others, not by the willingness to compromise on a deficient middle ground."[1]

I would argue the "middle ground" he speaks of is not just deficient, but in a crisis communications context, it ranges from disastrous, to duplicitous, to merely disappointing. The disaster scenario is a group of leaders from Company A in crisis sitting around a boardroom table deciding the company's response and it turns out to be so compromised in terms of the truth or the proper context that media and the public accuse the company of a cover-up. Once caught in a cover-up you are not just on a slippery slope, you are in quicksand and sinking fast, with no one offering to lend a hand to pull you up—on the contrary, most people are cheering as you sink.

Look at the BP Gulf oil spill. The deeper the oil company plunged with its crisis communications blunders the more gleeful people seemed to react on social media, celebrating BP's screw-ups. You may just seem duplicitous if media or the public perceive that you have torqued the facts to your own benefit. The disappointing element in all of this is that had you been straightforward with the public—arranged and communicated the facts in a way that reflected the public interest—you could have earned significant praise and brand loyalty for your company. Instead, by fitting the public stereotype of the large, unfeeling corporation obsessed only with self-defense, you have squandered the opportunity to enhance your reputation, cement customer loyalty, and even attract new customers. And that is disappointing.

There are many things that are problematic for crisis communications advisers to discuss publicly due to client confidentiality, non-disclosure agreements, and just good common sense. That makes it difficult to get into specifics on topics as sensitive as this one. But I will warn you that group dynamics, particularly at a time of crisis, can very easily lead you down this slippery slope of compromise.

I've seen it happen. In fact, in my view it is more the rule than the exception. Again, not because the people involved were inherently evil. Their reactions were perfectly normal, even common. They just didn't approach the crisis with the correct mindset, with a laser focus on reflecting the public interest at all times. Remember, when a crisis strikes your organization, you will go through feelings similar to the five stages of loss and grief: denial, anger, bargaining (which leads to compromise), depression, and acceptance. It is perfectly natural in a group setting that individuals will reflect, endorse and echo the feelings and opinions of others in the group, particularly in a workplace setting where you have been in the trenches with these people on a daily basis. Add to the mix the reality that your legal counsel on the issue is likely to be very defensive in nature, so as to limit your organization's legal exposure.

## Compromise is the Easy Way

Moving toward compromise is the natural, most frictionless, way to go. It's easy to just nod in assent, particularly given the extraordinary time crunch you are facing in the crisis and the need to get your communications out there immediately. Unless you have someone in the room—the CEO, the corporate communications head, or an external crisis communications consultant—to recalibrate the conversation and bring it back to the fundamental issues of public interest, in most cases organizations will tend toward shaping or compromising the facts to some degree.

The slope is slippery because on Day One you might have to shade the truth just a little bit. But by Day Three you could be pressed harder and what started out as a bit of shade is now becoming a solar eclipse. All the while there is the reality of leaks. It's virtually impossible to ever track down where a leak came from, much less the motivation the person had for doing it, but leaks are common—from employees, from competitors, from stakeholders, and even from law enforcement officials. The leakers are inevitably motivated by the opposite objective of your own—that is, they want a negative story and they want to heighten the controversy. That is why it is best to avoid this slippery slope of compromise entirely and get the whole story out yourself. It is the only way you can assure that you will be bulletproof to future attacks on your credibility.

> Avoid this slippery slope of compromise entirely and get the whole story out yourself.

Don't lie. There, I've said it. Winston Churchill probably never imagined a day when his famous statement that "a lie gets halfway around the world before the truth has a chance to get its pants on" would literally be true. But here we are. It seems obvious and unnecessary to repeat, but it's not actually. I am still shocked by how often lies continue to be told, considering how few get away with it. It's like being a modern day bank robber—really, given today's technology, do you still think that's the perfect crime?

How far do we have to look for an example? Not far at all. The 2013 "Lie of the Year" according to Politifact.com was President Barack Obama's mantra in stump speeches across the country about the new health care plan: "If you like your health care plan, you can keep it."[2] Not only was it untrue for millions of Americans, but evidence emerged (as it always does when you are caught in a lie) that the Department of

Health and Human Services had been telling the White House as far back as 2010 that substantial numbers of Americans would lose their existing health care plans under the new Affordable Care Act.

Worse, the Obama White House was accused of hiding behind the lie to get the Act passed by Congress. Now here's where the slippery slope comes into play: When the Democrats were accused of the Obamacare lie, they reacted by sliding further down the slope and assigning blame to obscure grandfathering clauses in the Act and blaming insurance companies. No matter, because once the feeding frenzy starts in today's always-on media environment, all sorts of embarrassing situations usually come to light.

Just one example: PBS *Newshour* interviewed a defense attorney named Deborah Persico of Washington, D.C., who was a supporter of the health care legislation until her policy was canceled and replaced with one with a significantly higher rate. Still, her new more expensive policy covered a few things her old policy did not, including pediatric services and maternity care. Except that Persico was 58 years old at the time. "I nearly fell off my chair," she told PBS, "because for years all I have heard from President Obama was, 'If you like your policy you can keep your policy, if you like your doctors you can keep your doctors.'"[3] Persico, who voted for Obama twice, said her former health insurance plan offered "perfect" coverage, while the new one befuddled her. "It will cost me, probably, $5,000 a year more than what I was paying for before," she said. "It was total sticker shock . . . as for maternity coverage and pediatric are, I am 58 years old. The chance of me having a child at this age is zero. So I ask the President, why do I have to pay $5,000 a year for additional maternity coverage that I will never use?"

*Huffington Post* political reporter Jason Linkins captured the situation effectively when he wrote, "I am one of those types of people who vastly prefers to be leveled with, as opposed to being shined on. But even I can see how one might prefer 'If you like your plan, you can keep it,' to 'When the law is implemented, it will vastly reshape the insurance market, which means a not-insignificant portion of the population will be dropped by their insurers or funneled onto plans that cost more, and not all of these people will end up finding their affordable opportunity on the new health insurance exchanges.' The latter statement's honesty is the sort of thing that sends political advisers screaming from the room."[4] Indeed. But it would have been honest and it would have insulated Obama and the Democrats from the kinds of withering character attacks that have occurred since the Act's passage—by everyone from political opponents to *Saturday Night Live.*

The number of Americans who said they distrust Obama shot up in public opinion surveys. By January 2014, the respected Quinnipiac University survey showed that 49 percent of Americans felt that Obama was not "honest and trustworthy," while 46 percent said he was.[5] Not only would a more honest approach likely have avoided such negativity in a mid-term election year, it would have also precluded the need for Obama to sit down with NBC's Chuck Todd for a full-blown interview at the White House, primarily to apologize to the American people.

When it comes to taking an honest, no-compromises approach to communicating about your crisis, it's worth better understanding the climate of deep mistrust you're stepping into and what that means for how you will be treated and perceived. One of the marketing pieces the big PR agencies use that I have always admired (and its competitors always envied, a little bit) is Edelman's Trust Barometer. The company has been doing it annually since 2000. The 2014 version is comprehensive. The company surveyed 33,000 people in 27 markets around the world about their trust in institutions, credible information sources and channels, and specific issues impacting trust in business and government. It found that trust in business had largely stabilized at 58 percent after a rocky 2008 during the financial crisis, whereas trust in government had plummeted.

Among businesses, technology-based and automotive companies were the most trusted, while banks were the lowest on the trust scale, including being near rock bottom in some countries such as Spain (16 percent), Italy (23 percent), the U.K. (32 percent), Germany (33 percent), and France (38 percent). Overall, family-owned small and medium-sized businesses were trusted more than large corporations (except in Asia). And while trust in CEOs had plummeted to just 31 percent in 2009, that group had recovered slightly to 43 percent. CEOs ranked the second lowest among the eight groups of individuals the survey asked about, just ahead of government officials (36 percent). Consider as a benchmark that 62 percent of respondents said they trust the category a "person like yourself"—in other words someone like your neighbor or your friend—and the top trust scores went to academics (68 percent) and technical experts (66 percent). Imagine if your child came home from school with these kinds of marks. There would likely be a remedial plan put in place to improve them.

## Notes

1. www.pon.harvard.edu/daily/conflict-management/questioning-compromises/
2. www.politifact.com/truth-o-meter/article/2013/dec/12/lie-year-if-you-like-your-health-care-plan-keep-it/
3. www.pbs.org/newshour/bb/government_programs-july-dec13-health_11-12/
4. www.huffingtonpost.com/2013/12/13/politifact-lie-of-the-year_n_4440120.html
5. www.quinnipiac.edu/news-and-events/quinnipiac-university-poll/national/release-detail?ReleaseID=1999

# Chapter 10

# A Thousand Tiny Cuts

ONE OF THE MOST troubling trends in crisis communications is that people tend to think about it only in the context of "the big one," the way people in California talk about that one huge earthquake they truly fear. They don't pay much attention to small tremors, other than a bit of water cooler talk—"Hey, did you feel that yesterday?" What I believe board directors, corporate executives, or leaders of other public and private sector organizations are missing—almost entirely—is the meaning of crisis communications or issues management tremors.

There tends to be a dismissive point of view when it comes to smaller issues. "Well, it didn't turn out to be much of an issue anyway. We didn't handle it particularly well, but it was a small issue and it was over quickly." Of course your brand can be destroyed in the giant explosion of a crisis that you fail to manage effectively, but it is also very common—more common actually—for brands to die a death by a thousand cuts. The term *death by a thousand cuts*, which has entered the vernacular, actually refers to a brutal form of torture causing a painful, lingering death that was used in Imperial China from about AD 900 until it was banned in 1905. You hear the term used often by crisis communications advisers to explain why, when a crisis strikes, you need to get all the negative information about the issue out quickly, in one day, so that you can have that "one bad day" and move on, rather than suffering death by a thousand cuts as more negative facts about the scandal leak out or are discovered gradually.

That's an accurate description of a crisis communications best practice, but it is not what death by a thousand cuts really means. What those advisers are referring to is just an example of a crisis that was poorly managed by the organization in the immediate to medium term. The more accurate description of death by a thousand cuts in terms of crisis communications is when organizations don't consider each instance—each small event—important enough to put proper resources against it. It's a more long-term, multi-year process where issues are swept under the rug, where patterns of poor communications, processes, and behavior become the norm. It should be referred to as Brand Death By a Thousand Cuts.

Veteran California-based (by way of Australia) marketer Al Nucifora, a Harvard MBA and frequent public speaker, has a great way of capturing the fascination he shares with many of us about why some brands slowly wither and die, and why some brands prosper in a lasting way. He writes about well-established brands, household names really, "that have experienced a slow, almost imperceptible wasting-away over time."[1]

What's essential about these brands is that no single event that occurs is considered in the context of potentially ruining the brand's reputation or putting it out of business. Instead, it's like suffering a small cut in the kitchen. You bandage it and move on, never thinking it could have a permanent impact on your health or possibly cause you to die. That's what people miss in terms of crisis communications and issues management. They also miss it in the context of internal employee communications, customer communications, stakeholder communications, and brand marketing.

Think about that cable and internet company that you deal with locally. Chances are there is one large, dominant provider. But if that provider keeps increasing the cost of its "channel packages," or doesn't provide strong technical support when customers' cable is knocked out, or has a poor billing support inquiries service, eventually customers will begin to explore their options, even if that means a smaller, less-tested competitor. That's why many of the top telecommunications companies fight the "small fights" on customer service and treat seemingly small issues with significance, because when you add them up, they are significant.

"Once infected, the patient sinks into an ever-worsening spiral which no amount of intensive care can arrest. Illness begets more serious illness until the patient ultimately dies," Nucifora writes. He references major airline companies Eastern and Pan Am as two examples, along with Radio Shack (a brand I loved as a teenager and would have never imagined dying), K-Mart, and Sears. Here's how he describes the typical chain of events: "Strained labor relations, exacerbated by a management mindset that is focused almost exclusively on economic survival, results in ever-worsening internal morale. Employees understandably obsess about their own well-being, lose faith in the company and turn surly, uncaring and cynical in the process. Their disdain for their livelihood clearly shows. The customer inevitably suffers in the process and elects to flee the brand.

"Why stay in a relationship where one is no longer appreciated or wanted? From management's perspective, life is a constant battle for survival. Rearguard actions are the order of the day. The company's attention turns inward and as the eye comes off the ball, the external focus is lost. Customer service turns lousy and established customer relationships begin to fray or come apart. Competition smells blood. Now it's just a countdown to the end."[2]

## When Innovation Wanes

In most cases these brands have not only long given up trying to fulfill the mission they initially created, he argues, they have also abandoned any pretense at innovation or freshness. That means these brands get old and stale, and don't draw any buzz or excitement around them, he says, as was the case with GM's Oldsmobile division. I believe that is why Ford is now working so aggressively trying to innovate and inject freshness into its luxury Lincoln brand, for example, following on the heels of some innovative new products from Cadillac that began to make Lincoln look old. We've witnessed it in the tech sector, too. When signs of this death spiral (or even signs of a downturn) begin to occur, the top talent flees for the hotter, more innovative workplace; top brains abandon Microsoft for Google, while Research in Motion (now the on-life-support Blackberry brand) loses its best and brightest to Apple or Samsung.

It also happens to cities. Let's take Detroit and Seattle as examples. I don't believe in the 1960s or 1970s as the U.S. auto manufacturing sector hummed along that anyone in prosperous Detroit was very worried about being overtaken by a city like Seattle, which had been known mostly for logging and shipbuilding. Even when it looked like Boeing Corporation would jumpstart the Seattle economy, the oil crisis hit, Boeing lost some government contacts and there were cost overruns on the 747 jets. People began to flee Seattle in droves, so much so, that in 1971 a local realtor put up a billboard in town that stated: "Will the Last Person Leaving Seattle Turn Off the Lights?"

Detroit, the Motor City, was still churning out big, gas guzzling cars that North Americans loved to drive on their new highways, and to work and back to homes in increasingly far-flung suburban subdivisions. Then came the first few cuts. Detroit's auto industry was dinged in 1973 when the gasoline crisis hit and foreign automakers who manufactured smaller, more fuel-efficient cars began to make inroads in North America. That trend continued in 1979 when the second gas crisis struck.

The truth was, Detroit was already witnessing a slow and steady decline that had begun in the late 1950s. The American auto industry wasn't really innovating, not to the degree of its foreign competitors. It was experiencing strained labor relations. Can you see the pattern we discussed above developing? Just as that second gas crisis hit Motown, Seattle saw a boon, as a fairly young company named Microsoft decided to relocate its headquarters to nearby Bellingham, Washington.

Soon the Seattle suburbs were populated by rising tech giants like Amazon, RealNetworks, and Nintendo, along with mobile phone companies that became part of giants AT&T and T-Mobile. There was a real buzz about Seattle. It was attracting the best and the brightest not just in the tech industry, but in the arts as well. Its population booming, Seattle's real estate became some of the most expensive in the country by the year 2000, just as Detroit was beginning to crash and burn.

As we all know, between the year 2000 and 2010, Detroit's population fell 25 percent. Even the bursting of the dot-com bubble didn't take the wind out of Seattle's sails, but by 2013 Detroit declared bankruptcy, owing more than $18 billion to creditors. The city once admired worldwide as the home of the U.S. auto industry now has the distinction of having filed the largest municipal bankruptcy in history.

Seattle, meanwhile, was riding high at a time when statistics showed that most 16-year-olds were in no hurry to get a drivers license or buy a car, and the kinds of tech gadgets they owned were their true indicators of social status. As many of them said: "Why do I need a car to drive to the movies, when I have a laptop and I can get my movie on Netflix?" And, to add insult to injury, Netflix is another West Coast success story, located down the coast from Seattle near San Jose, California.

Look at it this way, if you purchased an average American home in an average American city in the year 2003, it would have been worth 14 percent more by the year 2013, 10 years later (and that's with the historic U.S. housing market crash and financial crisis of 2008 factored in). If you bought that average house in Seattle, it would be worth 32 percent more, the highest jump among the 20 biggest U.S. cities. If you bought the average home in Detroit, it would be worth 23 percent less, by far the biggest drop of the major cities surveyed.[3]

## Reporter Inexperience Equals Errors

There are many who believe that journalism—and the journalists who will cover your crisis—is dying a death by a thousand cuts. Newspaper,

TV, and radio newsrooms have been through wave after wave of layoffs, buyouts, early retirement packages, and outsourcing in the last decade. When your crisis strikes, remember that newsrooms are in a position today where they need to produce the news faster, but do so with fewer resources. In the newspaper business, beating opponents once meant having a story in the printed newspaper in the morning that your opponent didn't have. In most cases, that translated into your newspaper being on sale all day long with your "scoop" over the competition. The other newspaper in town couldn't write a "matcher" or try to advance the same story until the next day.

In today's newspaper business, scoops or exclusives are measured in terms of mere minutes. When one newspaper breaks a story online, it is literally picked up in bulletin form (just a headline, with a note "more to follow") within minutes. It is tweeted within seconds.

But that mad rush to be first is also happening when you have far fewer editors in newsrooms fact-checking. Most of the older reporters and editors with institutional memory—those who would just "smell" that something wasn't right about a story—are long gone, the recipients of buyout packages and retirement bridges that leave them to a life of pursuits such as freelance writing, either for publications or for corporate writing assignments. Some even spend time on Facebook bemoaning the demise of the quality of the journalism business. At most newspapers, editors (the fact-checkers and people who catch typos and mistakes) have been among the first to be laid off.

In terms of how you will be covered when a crisis strikes your company, this is all worth keeping in mind because in newsrooms speed plus inexperience equals errors. That means you need to communicate twice as much, twice as clearly, and twice as quickly to ensure the reporter gets it right.

Talk about death by a thousand cuts, how about 18,400 cuts? That's the number of newspaper jobs lost in the U.S. between the year 2000 and 2012, according to the influential Pew Research Center, starting at 56,400 newspaper jobs in 2000, falling to 38,000 in 2012.[4] Remember, there are nowhere near 38,000 newspaper jobs in America today because the cuts have continued unabated.

The Pew Research Center's Project for Excellence in Journalism program states that consumers of mainstream media are leaving newspapers, TV, and radio news for the very reasons Nucifora described. Pew's Jodi Edna and Amy Mitchell wrote that although most of the 2,000 adults surveyed in 2013 by the organization weren't aware of the reasons for the financial cutbacks at news outlets, "a significant percentage of them not only have noticed a difference in the quantity or quality of news, but have stopped reading, watching or listening to a news source because of it. Nearly one-third—31%—of people say they have deserted a particular news outlet because it no longer provides the news and information they had grown accustomed to. . . . And those most likely to have walked away are better educated, wealthier and older than those who did not—in other words, they are people who tend to be most prone to consume and pay for news."[5]

## The Dribble of Bad News

General Motors, though not dead by any means, is one prominent corporation that some have argued has been suffering a thousand cuts in a crisis communications context. The so-called "deadly ignition switch" crisis has caused GM to recall 2.6 million small cars globally, mostly Chevrolet Cobalts and Saturn Ions. The cars have faulty ignition switches that have been plagued by problems of slipping out of the run position to "off," disabling airbags, shutting engines down (sometimes at high speeds), and removing the power assist functionality of steering and brakes, making the cars difficult to control.

As of May 2014, GM confirmed 13 deaths and 31 crashes linked to the switches. A Texas lawyer representing a number of plaintiffs said 53 people have been killed and 273 injured. The thousand cuts in this case involve ongoing revelations that GM has been aware of problems with the ignition switches for more than a decade, but didn't actually do recalls until 2014.

Let's count up the cuts: Report (*cut to GM's reputation*), after report (*cut*), after report (*cut*) have cited what GM knew and when it knew it. These are damning cuts because they imply GM knew of the dangers caused by the switches but rather than put the public safety interest first, the automaker put its own self-interest in profits first.

*USA Today* (March 23, 2014) reported a damning tale of a single word buried deeply in an investigator's report on a 2005 fatal crash involving a lovely young Maryland teenager who lost control of her Chevy Cobalt. When it slammed into a tree her airbags did not deploy and the force of the crash crushed her against the steering wheel, resulting in her death. Amber Marie Rose was pictured with her blonde ringlets and wearing a blue prom dress. She had sped away from a party after arguing with a boy. But what an investigator found at the crash scene was that her Cobalt ignition switch was in the "accessory" position, which is used only to power things like the car radio. Since she was driving the car, the switch would have needed to be in the "run" position for the engine to be running. Seeing this problem was consistent with past evidence of the switches slipping out of the run position, the investigator advised GM of the finding in 2007.

The *USA Today* story also pointed to GM being aware of problems with the ignition switches based on other evidence in 2004 (*cut*), 2005 (*cut*), and 2007 (*cut*), the latter when four crashes were linked to the switches slipping out of the run position, shutting off the engines, power brakes, and power steering, and disabling the airbags. In addition to hearings before Congress (*cut*), the National Highway Traffic Safety Administration (NHTSA) also announced an investigation (*cut*) of why GM delayed the recalls after being aware of the problem for so long. Then came the criticism that GM was using its 2009 bankruptcy (*cut*) to shield itself from legal claims that relate to accidents which took place before the July 2009 GM bankruptcy filing.

As the *New York Times* noted (*cut*), here was GM after 17 profitable quarters, its government loans fully repaid, suddenly back in bankruptcy court.[6] Why? To use a legal technicality to fend off these pre-2009 ignition switch lawsuits—a move purely in GM's own self-interest (*cut*). The two lead lawyers arguing GM's position before the bankruptcy court did not return calls from the *New York Times* (*cut*), a so-called "no comment" that cannot be allowed in crisis communications because it amounts to answering "guilty."

The Northeast Ohio Media Group ran an editorial cartoon that reproduced the blue GM logo with a coffin below the letters GM, while etched into the coffin were the words "Management Ethics" (*cut*). It wasn't until April 2014 that GM finally put two engineers on "leave"[7] (*cut*) as part of its own internal investigation of the issue, a move that was widely panned as far too little, far too late. GM then advised that it had found yet another defective part (*cut*) related to the ignition switches, this time the ignition lock cylinders. Then documents were released that prompted more than one nasty headline (*cut, cut, cut*) like this one from Reuters: "Documents Show GM's Sluggish Response to Deadly Defect."

It was reported that GM's stock hit a 10-month low (*cut*), just a few days after the NHTSA announced it had fined GM for failing to meet a deadline to supply information (*cut*) for its investigation. All of this after Senator Claire McCaskill told ABC's *This Week* that the "Justice Department is taking a hard look," at jail time for GM executives who may have perpetrated a decade-long cover-up (*cut*) of the faulty ignition switches.

I could go on with *cut* after *cut* after *cut*, but you get the picture. GM's reputation is in tatters and it will take some time (measured in years) to deliver the kind of very deliberate and transparent efforts required for the company to repair its reputation in the minds of millions of consumers.

What caused this? It wasn't one big catastrophic crisis. It was a series of crises, small ones, over a decade where GM ignition switch technology did not work. At the time of these mini-crises, GM officials may or may not have even noticed, nor added up the clues about the fact that something much bigger was going on. It's true that in the lead up to the July 2009 bankruptcy, GM executives were 100 percent engaged in fighting for the company's very life—negotiating with the government regarding a bailout loan and making survival decisions that not long ago would have been unfathomable, including jettison- ing entire brand lines with their own historic pedigrees like Pontiac and Oldsmobile. GM managers entrenched and focused on survival obviously missed some pretty big clues on the ignition switch issue.

> GM managers entrenched and focused on survival obviously missed some pretty big clues on the ignition switch issue.

## Small Compromises Equal Big Problems

And that is what death by a thousand cuts is all about—missed clues and a lack of focus. This is what we are talking about—the danger that as a company or organization, you are not paying close enough attention to these smaller events and the need to deal with them deci- sively before they turn into *cut* after *cut* after *cut*. As editors recently wrote in *BloombergView,* "The history of U.S. auto recalls is replete with unnecessary delays, refusals to make needed disclosures and managerial bungles. General Motors Co.'s recent recall of 1.6 million small-car models exhibits all three forms of corporate dysfunction."[8]

Organizations in situations like this (see our "slippery slope" dis- cussion) make what they think are small compromises with decisions entirely in the company's self-interest and opposite to the public interest. One small compromise leads to another, and another, and another. Soon you have a litany of examples of a company acting repeatedly and virtu- ally exclusively in its own self-interest—an indefensible position to be in when the crisis house of cards crumbles down on you. Once one media outlet exposes the issue you need to release everything you knew, all at once. GM did not do this. As a result, every single event from the past that indicated prior knowledge creates another cut. It only takes a half dozen or so of those and in today's media, you have a feeding frenzy.

## Losing "Control"

People talk about the need to "control" a crisis but most of those who try are the ones who end up losing control. Tiger Woods, the PGA Tour golfer, is a prime example of that truth. Few people, and among them I count presidents and prime ministers I covered as a journalist, held as tight a control over what was said and written about themselves and how their brand was presented to the world than Tiger Woods did up to November 27, 2009. I saw evidence of it first hand when I worked as Managing Editor of pgatour.com in Ponte Vedra Beach, Florida, at the TPC (The Players Championship) at Sawgrass. I didn't see everything first-hand, of course, because nobody did. The golfer and his powerful agents had reportedly shut down all sort of stories and shunned or intimidated media who wouldn't "play ball" with the world's most famous athlete. I did see clearly that, as he rocketed toward becoming the world's first $1 billion athlete, everyone wanted aboard the Woods train and they knew they needed to play by his rules.

Unfortunately, old habits die hard. Arrogance dies hard and humility sometimes comes too late in a crisis situation. Right from the beginning when Woods crashed his SUV into a tree outside his Florida home, the attempts to control the story were underway, with his wife Elin described as "heroically" trying to save him by bashing the rear windows of the Cadillac Escalade in with a golf club. I don't imagine anyone on Team Woods, much less Tiger himself, considered telling the truth at that point—after all, lies and intimidation had held for him up to this point.

Still, it only took one day for scandal site TMZ to report that Elin had scratched Tiger's face in a fight and that he crashed his SUV into a tree trying to flee their residence while she attacked the SUV with a golf club—all of this over an alleged affair Tiger had been involved in with a New York nightclub promoter, as reported by the *National Enquirer.*

A day later, now two days into the crisis, Woods released a vague statement that concluded with him saying it was a private matter and he wanted to keep it that way. Remember, Woods and those closest to him knew exactly what other sordid details could come out. But like they always had, they thought they could control it. This kind of arrogance is particularly acute in the million dollar world of professional sports—witness cyclist Lance Armstrong and baseball's Alex Rodriguez, to name a few.

Next came the thousand cuts for Woods: first a cocktail waitress, then a Las Vegas nightclub marketer. Now, about a week into his crisis, Woods decided to further control the situation by issuing a second media statement, this one going further than the first one by stating that he let his family down, ". . . and I regret those transgressions with all of my heart." Next up? Stories that Woods' camp paid off the New York nightclub promoter who started it all, followed by a fellow golfer whose family introduced Woods to his wife Elin saying he had lost all respect for Woods.

Then a blonde model named Jamie Jungers told the U.K. *Daily Mirror* of a two-year affair with Woods (Jungers would later become known as "Mistress #4" as a scorecard was required by that time); followed in short order by a model named Cori Rist, who alleged a two-year affair with Woods; and next was Mindy Lawton, described as an $8-per-hour diner waitress who had sex with Woods in his SUV. Then it really started going downhill for Woods.

Next out was a porn star named Holly Sampson. The very next story on deadspin.com alleged that the two nightclub promoters, one in New York and one in Las Vegas, also took on the duty of lining up women for Woods to have sex with when he was traveling to different cities. That story also introduced the world to someone who considered herself a "full-time" mistress of Woods, porn star Joslyn James.

About three weeks into this craziness more sponsors—including Gatorade, Accenture, Gillette, and Tag Heuer dropped Woods, while talk show hosts feasted on the story and much of the sports world, and certainly the professional golf community, was in shock. By mid-December there were reports in *The Globe and Mail* that the man who had helped Woods recover from several injuries was under investigation by the FBI in the U.S. and by the RCMP in Canada related to the alleged sale of performance-enhancing drugs.

Even with the feeding frenzy in full flight, the Woods team still tried to manipulate and control the situation. Media outlets were warned darkly about potential outcomes among advertisers who hadn't abandoned Woods yet. Even PR agencies whose top professionals were being asked by the media to comment on the Woods case were contacted and warned they could potentially lose corporate clients unless they ceased and desisted.

Meanwhile, it just got worse—predictably, because if you've slipped this far down the slope in a crisis there's no coming back. His wife Elin was said in reports at the time to be planning to divorce Woods. In late December AT&T ended its sponsorship agreement with the player. In mid-January 2010, General Motors announced that it would terminate its agreement with Woods—an agreement that included free access to their vehicles as well as the Buick insignia on Woods' golf bag.

Near the end of January a 19th woman was reported to have had an affair with Woods. It wasn't until February 19, 2010, almost three months into the crisis, that Woods finally conducted a "carefully orchestrated" media event at a Florida golf course to come clean about his affairs, talk about his counseling, and speak frankly about his family and the kind of man he wants to be.[9] He left without taking any questions from media. It was another month before Woods actually answered questions in a media interview.

The golfer was judged to have done a fairly good job taking ownership for his actions at the Florida media event. But it does beg the question of why Woods and his team let the crisis go on for three months, only to do the type of mea culpa event that he could have done much sooner and avoided months of self-serving denials and hiding out.

It's the attempts to flip off the crisis with those two earlier vague media statements that many now remember; the old Tiger who still believed—despite everything he knew he had done—that he could control the situation.

Woods had the equivalent of a several thousand reputational cuts over those three or four months. To many, his reputation will never recover.

## Notes

1. www.nucifora.com/art_303.html
2. Ibid.
3. www.nytimes.com/interactive/2011/05/31/business/economy/case-shiller-index.html?_r=0
4. www.pewresearch.org/fact-tank/2013/06/25/newspaper-newsrooms-suffer-large-staffing-decreases/
5. http://stateofthemedia.org/2013/special-reports-landing-page/citing-reduced-quality-many-americans-abandon-news-outlets/
6. nytimes.com, May 2, 2014
7. reuters.com. April 10, 2014
8. bloombergview. March 18, 2014
9. cnn.com. Feb. 19. 2010

# Chapter 11

# This Is Not a Test

ONCE YOU HAVE FACED A CRISIS and started to deal with it, the most important thing to remember is that this is not (primarily) about Public Relations. It's not about effectively executing on your impeccably planned crisis communications protocol. It's not about editing and revising and rewriting and reshaping and reformatting and reordering and rewording a press release to within an inch of its life. And it's not about getting out there and yelling as loudly as you can "We're the good guys!!!" As counter-intuitive as this is coming from a crisis communications expert, the most important element of what you do has absolutely nothing whatsoever to do with communications.

It's about the actual decisions you make. It's about whether you approach the situation focused on the public interest, or on your own self-interest. Exact protocols are fine but rarely executed exactly. It is true that people in your organization should have roles to play and should understand your protocols. But as we discussed earlier, there is no PR tactic that exists that can make a bad decision seem good—it's the proverbial lipstick on a pig. It's about doing the right thing, even if it is financially painful, or seemingly a step backwards, in the short-term. It's about making it right.

Forget about the drill, for now. There will be time—much later on—to evaluate how well your communications systems did or did not

> It's about whether you approach the situation focused on the public interest. Exact protocols are fine but rarely executed exactly.

work. This is not a test of the quality of your writing. Besides, good writing is invisible. It's only bad writing that stands out. I can tell you that how well-written your media statement or press release is plus-or-minus 1 percent of your crisis communications outcome. Yet I still see people in crisis situations spend 50 or 60 or even 70 percent of their time debating or editing a piece of paper that very few people will ever see. Even those who do see it, in the media, won't base their story on it anyway. Just get it out. Less is more. Ultimately focus on what will be plus-or-minus 90 percent of your outcome—the actions you take and whether or not you're doing the right thing.

There is no communications tactic that will elevate your company's reputation more effectively than making the tough decision and putting it into action. If a PR professional ever looks you in the eye and says: "Of course we can avoid a product recall because I can spin the media on it," fire that person immediately. Get security to escort them out the door.

North Americans have a very well-honed sense of fairness. If you apologize and do the right thing, there is an enormous capacity for forgiveness that awaits. But that's just table stakes. That is coming out of a crisis situation more or less level. If you want to define what you really stand for as a brand, if you want to grow and enhance your reputation, you need to go further.

Going further means shattering perceptions of your brand, or of the brand category you exist in. That's an area we'll explore. But first you need to take those concrete steps not only to "make things right," but to ensure that another incident or event isn't going to derail your organization's crisis recovery. While there is no substitute for doing the right thing, there is also no savior for failing again. This is not a baseball game where you can say, "Hey I only have one strike against me—I still have two more." In most crisis communications scenarios, this is a game of *2 strikes* and you're out. Particularly if the second strike comes within a very short time of the first strike.

Nothing will destroy your credibility and your brand faster, and more permanently, than screwing up again. The perception becomes ingrained that nothing you said after strike one was true, nor will anything you say going forward be true. Now is the time that you need to be flawless in your company's execution. Better to shut down the plant that produces your best-selling product and find out the source of the contamination than to sell another contaminated package after pledging it would never happen again. You need to deliver on your commitments and you need to re-establish trust by doing what you said you were going to do, step-by-step, as your brand slowly recovers.

## Apology and Acknowledgment

Step one is AA—sorry, not that one—we're talking about a proper apology and acknowledgment. Either one done halfway makes the entire situation worse. This is a critical moment because it is likely the first time the public has heard from you since the crisis broke open. If either of these two—the apology or the acknowledgment—are delivered in a less than fulsome and authentic fashion, it completely undermines the other.

Let's start with the apology. Much has been made of Southern foodie Paula Deen's three attempts at an apology for allegedly using the N-word with her staff. In my view, once the first apology failed the other two were doomed. Deen slipped into a pity party of self-interest and her handling of that personal crisis has now become a how-to-not-do-it staple of crisis communications lists.

What is the first ingredient of a successful apology? It is the main ingredient Deen was missing: remorse. To say you are sorry, you have to actually *be* sorry. Throughout this book you will see references from me to debunking the notion that there is some sort of "secret sauce" to crisis communications, some art form that can be learned over many years like a doctorate. Not so when it comes to apologizing. You need to get

> To say you are sorry, you have to actually *be* sorry.

yourself to the place where you understand how the injured party or parties feel in terms of the crisis you or your company caused.

An apology is not a brush-off. Unfortunately today, it has become a conversational tool frequently and flippantly tossed out: "I'm sorry," then bridge to your argument—as in, "I'm sorry you feel that way, *but the point is . . .*" As we all know, that person isn't sorry at all, just argumentative. The other non-apology apology is the tried and (un) true: "If that's the way you feel, I am sorry that you feel that way and I apologize." Look, this isn't an over-heated fight with your spouse. It's a crisis on which the future reputation of your company or organization hinges, and likely on which your immediate career prospects also hinge.

Third, an apology should never be viewed by you as an appeasement. "Let's do this apology and it will die down." That's also not remorse. It's self-serving just to want the people complaining to go away and leave you alone.

## The Pizza Apology

Case in point: Chevron. Back in winter 2014, residents of the rural community of Bobtown in southwestern Pennsylvania heard a thunderous explosion. It was caused by the nearby Chevron fracking well that had exploded. One worker was killed, and the community watched in horror as flames shot into the sky. It was a dangerous fire that took five days to extinguish. Residents kept hearing a constant hissing sound and worried about toxins that might be released into the air.

What did traumatized area residents receive from Chevron? A note with a coupon in it for one large pizza and one two-liter bottle of soda, if redeemed by May 1st. The Chevron letter contained no apology, just an "update" and a commitment to safe operations. Among the snarky and sarcastic social media responses when the story went viral was the fact that it was understandable that the offer was for only a standard pizza and local residents could not customize their toppings because after all, Chevron's net income for 2013 was only $21.42us billion, off $4.76 billion from the previous year. Plus, keep in mind, as the 2010 Census revealed, Bobtown's population was 757 people.

Was it any surprise then that the "pizza apology" itself became the crisis, not just nationally, but internationally? Not the actual explosion. The apology. *Philadelphia Daily News* columnist Will Bunch said the situation offered a new marketing slogan for Chevron: *"We guarantee your fracking rig won't explode, or your pizza is free!"*[1] Of course the pizza and soda wasn't the entirety of Chevron's response. It actually has a community relations program in that area, staffed by people who, one assumes, although well-intentioned should have known better.

Finally, an apology needs authenticity. The standard was set not just in terms of authenticity, but in terms of delivering video apologies, in 2007 by then-jetBlue CEO Dave Neeleman, who spoke from the heart about stranding some of his passengers during an ice storm, how much he regretted it, and how he intended to ensure it would never happen again. He wore a plain white shirt and, standing, looked right into the camera, speaking conversationally, but seriously, and most impor-tantly—not off of a script.

Another video apology came that year from then-Mattel CEO Bob Eckert after the company recalled 9 million toys manufactured in China due to unsafe levels of lead. Eckert, in a suit and tie, sat down and delivered a more scripted response. Still, the content was comprehensive in terms of Mattel's reforms and Eckert's own personal commitment to safety. Importantly, Eckert didn't rule out the possibility that Mat-tel might have to recall more toys, but he did vow to tell consumers promptly if that happened.[2]

But somewhere along the line, crisis communications apologies went off the rails. Like the Chevron pizza incident, many CEO apologies have been considered, at best, flaccid, and at worst, offensive. The primary reason is a lack of sincerity. While we've discussed the inherent decency of North Americans and their sense of fairness and willingness to forgive, let it also be said that the public is cunning about sniffing out a fake.

Not to mention that social media types salivate to expose that fakery, and never more so than when it comes to a less than stellar crisis apology.

One brutal video apology came from then-RIM co-CEO Mike Lazaridis following the Fall 2011 global outage Blackberry users suffered. The apology was considered late (four days into the crisis) and it reeked of insincerity, with Lazaridis clearly delivering a heavily scripted message that he appeared to read from something just to the right of the camera lens, his eyes darting back and forth. The content was there, but the sincerity wasn't and RIM paid the price.

Former Lululemon CEO and founder Chip Wilson's video apology also rang hollow primarily because he talked more about how he felt and how the crisis created by his remarks about women's bodies had affected the employees of the company—and he talked less, in fact hardly at all, about the millions of women he had offended and how they must have felt.[3] In fact, when you enter the words "worst apology ever" into the YouTube search engine, Chip Wilson is No. 1.

Once you get the apology right—and I urge you to think long and hard about it, because the stakes are very high—you need to move on to the acknowledgment of what happened. This is where you have the opportunity to share how you feel about it in an authentic way—Are you angry? Are you crestfallen? Are you in shock? Be real. People who care enough about your crisis to be watching, listening to, or reading your comments about it are likely sharing some of those emotions and they want to be able to share that feeling with you and your organization.

We're not talking about a group hug here, but we are talking about your demonstrating that you care about what happened and that you are thinking about the people affected. Again, it is about shattering preconceived notions people have about you. If you are a corporate leader, the public may think you are incapable of real emotions or feelings. As crazy as that sounds, it is true. When lives have been lost in tragedies people don't want to hear from some kind of corporate robot spewing lines carefully crafted in the mahogany-paneled boardroom of some big law firm. They want to see the leader of the organization roll up his or her sleeves and get out among the people to share those emotions and bring comfort. That is a very real role you play.

If you think you or your CEO are incapable of doing this, get some help from a PR professional. When a crisis strikes a community or group of people initially they are in a very fragile state. And what they really want to hear is an acknowledgment of the magnitude of what just happened, a validation of the pain they are feeling. That empathy must come first, before your attempts to re-secure brand loyalty. Your response must come 100 percent from a public interest perspective. I cannot stress that enough.

## The Essential Extra Step

How, then, do you go about taking that extra step to shatter the public's preconceived notions? Let's break that down. We all know that a preconceived notion exists when people make their minds up about an issue without considering the evidence or facts of the matter. Most preconceived notions are based on stereotypes, for example: All politicians are ego-maniacs with questionable morals;[4] you cannot trust the media;[5] or, since you are not a mechanic, chances are you will get ripped off when you get your car fixed at the shop.[6]

Every city has a neighborhood with a certain reputation, so much so that when you hear about a person from that neighborhood, you may attach certain characteristics to that individual, even if you have never met the person. It sounds crazy at face value, but it's extremely common for people to rely on their preconceived notions in a world plagued by information overload.

How these stereotypes impact crisis communications is fairly obvious. When a cruise ship is stranded and passengers are enduring a hellish few days with no power, little food, and unsanitary conditions, people tap into their preconceived bias against either the cruise line companies or travel agencies in general. "They just don't care about their customers when things go wrong," people think. You can cite all the statistics and information available to show that the vast majority of people, in the vast majority of cases, have trouble-free vacations. But it doesn't matter. Media don't report on every plane that lands safely at the international airport, but the minute one crash-lands there is a palpable public buzz about how unsafe air travel is—despite the fact that it's statistically more dangerous to get behind the wheel of our cars.

That's why I recommend you do some research—not just about your own company's reputation, but the reputation and public attitudes towards your sector. Some outstanding consulting work is now being done by a few of the big international PR firms like FleishmanHillard. You can see research that maps where your company sits in terms of reputation against how the public and stakeholders view your sector as a whole. Ultimately, what that sort of research, along with focus groups, your own stakeholder mapping, and one-on-one outreach by your executive team, will tell you today is where your vulnerabilities are should a crisis strike.

## Be Bold

Understanding these realities is the first step to shattering preconceived notions by the public or your customers have about how you will act during a crisis. I advocate you take at least one hour in the earliest moments of the crisis as a management team to ask yourself two questions:

1) How does the public expect us to react to this based on their preconceived notions?

2) In doing the right thing here, how could we go above and beyond to shatter that perception of our company or organization?

I believe the conversation could point you in some interesting directions and ultimately lead you to swiftly and decisively take a step nobody predicted: one that is memorable for its boldness and its roots firmly planted in the public interest. Those are the kinds of outcomes that seize on the opportunity side of a crisis scenario.

Let me give you an example. A publicly owned Corporation A is the recipient of a freedom of information request for certain financial records. The freedom of information authority in that jurisdiction rules that, given the time it will take to pull all of these records, the applicant must pay a fee of several thousand dollars (to cover Corporation A's costs) in order to receive the information the law entitles that person to obtain. The local newspaper discovers what is happening and writes a story full of outrage about the fact that the fee of several thousand dollars is so high that it effectively amounts to barring this individual, or any member of the public, from obtaining information to which they have a legal right. This puts Corporation A into an issues management scenario that could potentially become a crisis. It could be one of the thousand cuts that impacts Corporation A's overall reputation.

There are two choices: Ignore the issue and hope the media and other commentators do not champion it and make it into a much bigger issue (the head-in-the-sand approach), or take this head on in order to illustrate management's long-held commitment to accountability and transparency. So what do they do?

Senior management at Corporation A asks each other what they think the public would expect them to do: to hide behind bureaucracy and arcane rules to deny the release of the financial information; to operate secretively because (they suspect) there is some damaging information about wasteful spending that needs to be kept hidden. Senior management at Corporation A then asks each other what they could do to shatter those preconceived notions and help the public understand that their commitment to transparency is very real; what action would have a positive impact have on Corporation A's reputation?

The answer was clear: Release all of the financial information immediately, not just to the applicant, but to the public at large by posting it online for everyone to see and do this without charging any fees or cost to anyone. Corporation A went back to the journalist and explained the decision, which became big news and drew positive comments and reviews on social media.

There is still no secret sauce involved here. Corporation A did the right thing. The freedom of information law created to help shield publicly owned agencies and corporations from the costs of multiple information requests was well-intentioned, but it was always going to be possible for the organization involved to waive the fee. It was the right thing to do in this case and it shattered the expectation of the information applicant, the journalist who'd made the story into a controversy, and the public who read the story on the front page of the next day's newspaper.

Another example. Hospital A was conducting a random audit of its morgue when what was discovered was anything but routine. The body of a former patient, whose family thought had been picked up for cremation, and in fact been cremated, was mistakenly still in the morgue. The deceased's family, including parents, had largely already dealt with the grief related to the death of their loved one. But this was a major, major mistake that took place because a process broke down between those who administered the hospital morgue and the transportation company charged with moving people to a funeral home or crematorium.

One impulse Hospital A management had was to do all the right things with regard to an investigation into why this happened and how procedures could be put in place to ensure it never happened again, but to keep the information secret from the family, so as to avoid causing additional grief, particularly to the parents.

The judgment here was whether this was really the best process for the family, or whether it was a self-interested course of action that was designed to be easier for the hospital and to avoid the possibility that the mistake was made public?

It is said that the best issues managers and the organizations most adept at crisis communications are the ones you never hear about. That is true. But management of Hospital A also had to consider one chilling reality: If the body was transported and cremated now, and the family was not told, and then this story leaked out to the press afterwards, it would be devastating to the hospital's reputation—likely a blow that would take decades to overcome.

On the flip side, what could Hospital A do that would really shatter the public's expectation of how a hospital would act in these circumstances? It was obvious, but it also required bravery by the hospital's senior management team. The hospital CEO and a counselor who worked with the family went to visit the parents at their home one day for coffee. The CEO sat with the parents and fully explained what had happened. There was a vow to get to the bottom of it and to put measures in place that would ensure it never happened again. There was complete transparency. The CEO told the parents they could ask any question and it would be answered. By the time Hospital A's CEO was standing in the doorway of the house saying goodbye, there were hugs and there were tears. It never became a media issue and there was never the need to hide anything going forward.

They did the right thing. The parents deeply appreciated the honesty, the sincerity and the transparency. It was the right thing to do, but by going directly to the parents' home, it was above and beyond the expectation of what a busy CEO would do. Even if no one ever knows—as was the case here—it is more than just good karma for you and your organization; it is a good habit to get into. Do the right thing. Surprise people. Don't just talk about the principles your organization stands for. Demonstrate them with your actions.

> Do the right thing. Surprise people. Don't just talk about your principles. Demonstrate them.

There are other, more public, examples, but sadly they tend to be the exception as opposed to the rule. Tesco, the innovative U.K. supermarket chain, rapidly recalled all of its ground beef and immediately made a spokesperson available to media when the horsemeat scandal hit Britain in 2013.[7] In addition, CEO Philip Clarke used his blog to play back to customers what he thought their expectation of Tesco was in a situation like this: "Trust is hard won and easily lost. Our customers trust us that, if something goes wrong, Tesco will go above and beyond what is merely necessary to look after customers and will do the right thing, immediately and wholeheartedly."

What's required here to get a company or organization to the point where it is able to execute on something that shatters expectations is a mindset. You cannot have a CEO who is peevish because he or she feels like the company is being beaten up by the press. You cannot have a management team that is defensive. Your organization cannot be focused primarily on self-interest. Your organization cannot prioritize short-term issues over your reputation in the long term.

In the end it comes down to the most simple principle. Think about the public interest. Put yourself in their shoes. Think about the last time you were bumped off a flight by an airline, or one of your insurers denied you coverage. Think about the frustration you felt.

## Notes

1. www.prdaily.com/crisiscommunications/Articles/Chevron_apologizes_for_fracking_well_explosion_wit_16133.aspx

2. www.youtube.com/watch?v=xH9O8JlvOe4 http://www.youtube.com/watch?v=xH9O8JlvOe4

3. www.washingtonpost.com/posttv/entertainment/lululemon-founder-apologizes/2013/11/13/834f2a18-4c64-11e3-9890-a1e0997fb0c0_video.html

4. usatoday.com. Jan. 1, 2014

5. Gallup Poll. Sept. 21, 2012

6. https://ca.finance.yahoo.com/news/how-to-avoid-being-ripped-off-when-servicing-your-car-142909540.html

7. www.business2community.com/public-relations/supermarkets-set-the-standard-in-horsemeat-crisis-communication-0408976#!JN6MZ

# Chapter 12

# I've Seen This Movie Before

IN SURVEYS AND STUDIES, and in speeches and interviews, business leaders across North America and the world say that one of the top concerns keeping them awake at night is the sudden onslaught of a major crisis and questions that flow from that about how their organization would, in theory, respond.

A majority of leaders say that they either don't have a comprehensive crisis communications plan in place or they're not confident in the plan they do have. And among those who do have a crisis communications strategy nailed down, roughly one-third fear that their organization won't be able to execute it when the actual crisis strikes.

For example, PricewaterhouseCoopers' 2013 Annual Corporate Directors Survey polled members of corporate boards on the issue. It found that 41 percent of directors wanted to allocate more time to the organization's crisis communications protocols and planning, while almost 1-in-3 (29 percent) said they don't fully understand what their organization's crisis plan consists of.

Given what we know about how rapidly crises spread and how devastating they can be for an organization or brand, these numbers are still way too high. In terms of awareness, crisis communications has come of age, so to speak, in that it is portrayed in modern media (TV shows, movies) and is often discussed on social media and among professional journalists. But there is still a dangerous lag between the realization of its importance and actual steps taken by public and private sector organizations to prepare for the inevitable.

The truth is that these studies also uniformly show that most organizations don't create a crisis plan, or update the one they have to reflect today's realities and their most current business model, until *after* an actual crisis occurs. That's like saying "I'm going to buy home insurance," *after* your house burns to the ground. It's like when Bill Murray's character, Phil, in the movie *Groundhog Day* says to Rita, played by Andie MacDowell: "Do you know what today is?" "No, what?" she replies. "Today is tomorrow. It happened."

My first rule of creating an effective crisis communications plan is simplicity. The fatal flaw in plans that are in place for organizations is that they are far too detailed and multi-layered, resulting in two outcomes: 1) the plan isn't followed because at the speed a crisis takes its unpredictable twists and turns, it is quickly abandoned by core decision-makers, or 2) the organization's leadership insists the plan is followed to the letter and it slows the crisis response to a crawl, making the organization appear uncaring, out of touch, or just plain incompetent.

There is a great story about this—involving another movie starring Tom Hanks no less—from Washington-based communications leader B. J. Talley. Hanks starred in the Academy Award–nominated film *Captain Phillips,* about the first pirate hijacking of a U.S. ship in nearly 200 years. When the actual crisis took place in 2009, Talley was General Manager, Marketing and Communications for the Maersk Line Ltd, the company that owned the hijacked container ship the *Maersk Alabama.* What's telling in an article Talley wrote for the Public Relations Society of America is what he learned from the experience: "Build a process, not a plan."[1]

He expanded with what I consider excellent advice: "One of the most important things that I learned from the *Maersk Alabama* incident is that you can rarely predict the type of crisis that will happen. Prior to April 2009, like many PR professionals, I had a large binder in a desk drawer that contained my 'crisis plan.' It included a checklist and a set of key messages for what I believed could most likely impact my organization at the time. In this instance, our crisis turned out to be something that had not happened in more than 200 years—pirates hijacking an American commercial cargo vessel in international waters and taking its captain hostage. While there were some items in that binder that proved to be useful, we developed the vast majority of our tactics on the fly. That's why I recommend creating a crisis process and implementing tools that you can apply to any situation, rather than having a traditional, prescriptive crisis plan."

## The Importance of Simplicity

Seemingly endless attention has been paid to how badly BP managed crisis communications during the Gulf oil spill, but very little attention has been paid to how convoluted and poorly set up the overall communications management of the 2010 accident was. In their book *Effective Crisis Communications,* authors Robert R. Ulmer, Timothy L. Sellnow, and Matthew W. Seeger (Sage Publications, 2nd ed., 2010) paint a portrait of the confusing array of organizations dealing with the worst environmental disaster in U.S. history: The U.S. Coast Guard and the federal Bureau of Energy Management formed a partnership with BP to respond to the crisis.

They were, in turn, supported by more than a dozen federal agencies including the Department of Homeland Security, the Department of the Interior, the Fish and Wildlife Service, the National Institute for Occupational Safety and Health, and several others. A United Area Command (UAC) managed the response—it was comprised of four sectors (are you dizzy yet?) each reporting directly to the UAC. As the authors pointed out, part of this unified command structure involved Public Information Officers (PIOs). (As a side note, I am surprised there wasn't a unit called United Acronym Control, except its acronym would have clashed with the UAC.) It was the job of the PIOs to receive information about what was going on with the spill and then share that information with media and stakeholders—much like any public information office does at a time of crisis.

As the authors noted, the people who served as PIOs during the Deepwater Horizon crisis later said they "wished they had developed a unified communication plan or approach before the crisis or very early on during the event." Instead, different PIOs described themselves as having different objectives. Keep in mind that these were outstanding and experienced communications people brought in from all over the world—the best and the brightest. Still, they reported, ". . . challenges in meeting the constant onslaught of media requests, often aggressive questioning and demands for access . . . the waves of media requests, the dynamic nature of the crisis and the considerable amount of media made perfection difficult."

You can see how complexity was the enemy here—and it was reflected in the mixed messages and impressions of confusion and disarray that came out the Gulf during that 87-day crisis.

So start simply: The core crisis group needs to consist of your CEO, your VP or Director of Corporate Communications (depending on how your organization titles that lead position) and your in-house legal counsel. It's as simple as that. They are the "executive" of the crisis team, with the CEO heading it.

Add to that your head of Operations, your head of Human Resources, your Sales and Marketing VP, and your head of Public Affairs (government and stakeholder relations). Each should be responsible for their own channels. For example, the sales and marketing vice president should work with the marketing communications people on staff. If those people use a PR agency to provide primarily consumer-based PR programs, that agency should be brought into the mix even if they do not have expertise in crisis communications. You don't want to be seen to be callously conducting some kind of shiny-happy consumer PR promotion at the same time that some of your customers have been tragically impacted by a crisis related to your product. And keep in mind, any good consumer or brand-focused PR agency, if it values your business, will recommend to you a strong crisis communications expert who can be brought in to assist.

If your vice president of corporate communications already uses a PR agency on the corporate side, you should inquire as to what they can offer you in terms of a process for establishing a crisis communications plan. Often, companies that are planning ahead and realize the desperate need for a crisis plan actually conduct a Request For Proposal (RFP) and issue it to agencies that offer crisis counsel. This allows your company to evaluate several proposals in terms of what they involve, which expert advisers you will have access to in the event a crisis strikes, and the associated costs.

Most large companies also have agencies (we refer to them as "GR firms") with which they contract to provide government relations counsel. If so, your head of Public Affairs should bring those people into the loop as part of your crisis plan as well. If you are a small or mid-sized company that doesn't have an external GR agency and doesn't do much government relations, I still recommend you inquire through your own networks on who might advise you because communicating effectively with government during your crisis will save you untold headaches both in real-time and down the road.

Similarly, your in-house counsel will likely want to plan to involve the best and the brightest from the law firm that represents your company or organization.

All of these external advisers should be consulted in the creation of your crisis plan. And, as part of the plan, it should be made clear exactly who among those advisers will actually be seated at the table with your senior team when the crisis is on, because external counsel and perspective will be a key ingredient to your success.

Most large multi-national corporations conduct RFPs and award "agency of record" status to a PR firm to provide ongoing crisis communications, issues management, and reputation management counsel, often on a global basis. The large multinational PR firms like Edelman, Hill + Knowlton, FleishmanHillard, and Weber Shandwick, to name a few, have all developed their own proprietary crisis communications processes. Each offers value. One firm, Ketchum, even launched a crisis communications smart phone app in Spring 2014. If your organization is large enough it should consider what these firms and their local offices have to offer.

However, my advice is to ask for very specific information about the people who will work on your crisis, in addition to the crisis template the agency offers. The people are critical. As Talley pointed out above, just having the plan or process in place is useful. Training is useful. Knowing who is doing what is useful. But what I can assure you is that during the crisis, from Day One until you are in recovery mode, you will be forced to make judgment calls. Having experienced crisis counselors sitting at the table with you is invaluable.

You know your organization and what it does inside out. But you lack perspective. Often, you lack context. You're just too close to the situation. The benefit of having external crisis communications counsel is that they've worked in situations like this many times. They work fast. They can anticipate what the media wants next; many of them, in fact, are longtime former journalists. And they don't have a vested interest. Their career trajectory at your company is not impacted by the kind of counsel they provide in the crisis communications war room, because in all likelihood when the acute phase of your crisis ends, these senior advisers from an agency will be gone, off to the next assignment.

For that reason, you should also know that many of the top crisis advisers have left the so-called "big agency" world and set up their own companies. That is not necessarily an advantage to you as a client. Most of the success the independent boutique crisis communications companies have is determined by the level of expertise and brand recognition of the crisis communications expert it was likely named after. What happens if that person is unavailable when your crisis strikes? That's why you need to very carefully examine and question external crisis communications partners about the "people" part of any agreement you might reach.

The big PR agencies tend to have deeper benches, to use a sports analogy. But some of them are also known for higher fee structures. And in your market, there might be one specific crisis communications person who you just know you want on your side when the worst happens. This person may work for an agency large or small, or have started his or her own company. My advice would be to create an ongoing issues management relationship—a partnership—with that person in your market. Take advantage of the individual's media and government contacts. Chances are this individual can also vet your consumer marketing campaigns for potential crisis potholes or provide valuable insights into your government relations strategy. Then, when the crisis strikes, it is much more likely that no matter what that crisis expert is doing when your sky falls, he or she will drop it to be by your side.

## Planning the Process

So what needs to be in your crisis communications plan, or process? Again, keep it simple. The first thing everyone needs to understand is also something simple: What is the process required to make a decision and get something out the door. You would be surprised at how many organizations have a three-inch thick binder outlining an extremely detailed crisis plan and protocol, but once the crisis begins, nobody seems clear on when a decision is final or what the actual approval process is.

Your crisis responses and actions cannot be held up by bureaucracy —that would amount to a certain Twitter *#crisisfail*. So make Job #1 a clear statement of your approval process. It could be CEO sign-off only for all external-facing statements. Or, it might be more efficient to have a 2-in-3 setup for approval of things such as social media content, where two of the following three individuals have signed off: the vice president of corporate communications, the in-house counsel, and the head of operations. Some companies will have that 2-in-3 or 3-in-5 senior executive approval rule, but will stipulate that the general counsel must be one of the approvals.

Those on the approval committee need to clearly understand and accept the need for them to be available at all times during the crisis. Nothing will demoralize your team more quickly than to have an excellent crisis response initiative prepared and ready to go out, only to fail to get it approved in a timely fashion and then be widely criticized in mainstream media or on social media for being disorganized and slow to respond.

However, do not compromise on the approval process in the name of pure speed. Speed kills, particularly if it misses key considerations, like sensitivity.

Consider the Malaysian Airlines case in winter 2014, when the world's media descended on the story upon learning that the airline's flight MH370, with 12 crew and 227 passengers from 14 countries on board, had disappeared from the sky less than an hour after takeoff. The airline knew that families of those on board would soon be hearing from media that their loved ones were presumed dead.

So in the interest of timely crisis communications Malaysian Airlines sent a text message to the families: "Malaysia Airlines deeply regrets that we have to assume beyond any reasonable doubt that MH370 has been lost and that none of those on board survived. As you will hear in the next hour from Malaysia's Prime Minister, we must now accept all evidence suggests the plane went down in the Southern Indian Ocean." The use of a text message was widely slammed, as was the message's absence of any condolence. There was zero comfort and support. Zero offer of who to contact for more information or where to obtain resources or help families in this situation would desperately need.

Here's my take: You cannot tell me that a major airline that boarded more than 13 million passengers in 2011, generating revenues in excess of $4.5us billion, couldn't find 50 employees, put them in a call center with a prepared message, and have each of them call five families. Even if those families could not be reached by telephone, presumably the Malaysia Airlines employees could have left a message. A text message could have been used simply as a backup to ask the family member to call back as soon as possible on a toll-free line.

Once you have a clear approvals process, the first step is not to find out what happened, as some would have you believe. The first step, without hesitation, is to communicate immediately with those affected to apologize and acknowledge (as discussed earlier). Those affected, and the broader public and media, need to know right away that you are "on it."

> The first step, without hesitation, is to communicate immediately with those affected.

## Fill the Glass

You don't need all the answers with regard to how the crisis happened, or how the mistake was made. You might not even have all the facts yet. Nor should you guess or pre-judge what happened. But you should make a very firm commitment—after your apology—to gather every scrap of information and share it with those impacted. Then you should also make a clear commitment to implementing rules and regulations, checks and balances, which would prevent a reoccurrence.

And, finally, you need in this initial communication to put timelines on two things:

1) Exactly when and how you will be updating the public via the media on a regular basis.

2) How long you think it will take to at least have a preliminary answer as to what went wrong.

Put this process in place and then live by it—keep your commitments with regard to timing. Nothing enhances your reputation more as a company or organization during a crisis than committing to regular media updates at scheduled times, and then living up to that commitment. There should be no excuses for deviating from the schedule. If you don't have answers ready for that day's media briefing, or that morning's, or afternoon's, or evening's, media briefing, just say so and advise when you expect to have the answer. Keep to your schedule. It's all about being in control.

In the PR world, we often talk about the need to "fill the glass." It once meant something else for those of us who worked in the daily newspaper business in the 1980s and 1990s. But what we mean by this today is that, during a crisis, if you do not fill the glass in terms of content, someone else will fill it for you. During a crisis, if someone else fills it for you, it will invariably be a painfully negative experience for you—so do everything you can to fill it yourself.

The first way to do that is through your media briefings. If you are remotely located, meet the media's needs with regard to these briefings. Set up an on-site media briefing area with facilities to allow reporters to file their stories—essentially a place to sit with power and a fast DSL internet connection (coffee doesn't hurt, either). Of course this is less critical if you are doing briefings downtown in a major city and reporters are just a cab ride from their offices. If you are located in an extremely remote location, look at conference calls or other internet-based options that allow reporters from various locations to join the briefings.

In parallel to these breaking news media briefings, your process should also allow for journalists who are unfamiliar with what your company does, or your sector, to be briefed on background (not for attribution by name) by technical employees of your company.

But keep in mind, everyone who will come in contact with media, whether they have clearance to speak for the organization or not, needs to be media trained.

There are other ways to fill the glass. We know that visuals are absolutely essential to what TV does, so provide visuals. If you know that reporters are going to be regularly doing "stand-ups" or "live hits" outside of your headquarters, run a power line out to them to allow them to plug in, then position them in a dedicated area where the visual backdrop for those TV stand-ups is attractive, potentially with your name and logo.

Consider your online presence. Many organizations prepare what are known as "dark sites" for crisis communications purposes. These are websites that are not live on the internet, but can go live at the press of a button to provide a place affected individuals can go for regular information updates.

Having background materials at the ready also helps fill the glass, including broadcast-quality "b-roll" video of what goes on inside your facility. Remember if you are a food processor, for example, your plant may be shut down, making it impossible for TV to obtain these kinds of visuals. Absent that piece of video alone, TV journalists are more likely to go to one of your critics and ask them to go on camera.

Of course, given your ongoing stakeholder relations work, you should also be able to direct reporters to third-party commentators who are familiar with your company or your sector. All of this will contribute to getting your message out in a timely and accurate way.

Finally, in terms of process, it is critical that your crisis plan lay out a few basic internal protocols. The first one should be what time your internal crisis team will meet in the morning—assuming you are sleeping between days. It should be as early as possible. Second, you need to have a system set up for media monitoring (including broadcast—for radio and TV, the monitoring should produce transcripts) and for social media monitoring that will pull a report that can be distributed prior to that first morning meeting. The report should not be a dump of all the media coverage and social media commentary, but a summary by an experienced PR person that gives the top-line information on volume, tone (positive or negative), themes of the content, or new developments and any factual errors or omissions that need to be addressed. The report should serve to bring everyone on the crisis team fully up to date to start the day, so that at that first meeting, it can be reviewed and the crisis team can then move on to the day's priorities.

Don't find yourself scrambling to set up these internal systems and protocols when the crisis has begun. Getting quotes for social media monitoring and putting the people in place to execute protocols are process-driven issues you shouldn't have to spend time on when the crisis is at hand. The same goes for your internal communications processes, and the process for managing call volumes, which will inevitably spike at your call center.

Nail down as many of these internal processes in advance as you can, and then have clear accountability as to who is responsible for each area during the crisis itself. That will allow you to focus on the unforeseen crisis developments that are headed your way.

### Note

1. www.prsa.org/Intelligence/TheStrategist/Articles/view/10380/1084/Navigating_the_High_Seas_What_Somali_Pirates_Taugh#bio

# Chapter 13

# Dazed and Confused:
# Our Friends in the Media

THIS CHAPTER is very personal to me.

It is, by far, the hardest part of this book to write—and I say that as someone who has been churning out copy now for almost four decades. It causes me great pause because there is already plenty of advice (of varying quality) out there about media relations. I want to share something meaningful with you because these are the people you will encounter when your crisis strikes. It's worth understanding what they do.

I am both saddened by what has happened, and worried about what is about to happen, to journalism. It has been the one constant throughout my life, from the time I started writing about sports for the *Burlington Post* weekly newspaper when I was 15, until shortly after I covered the ceremony at Ground Zero that marked the first anniversary of the 9/11 attacks, as the Washington bureau chief for the *Toronto Star*.

It was all I ever wanted to do. For some of us, you just know from a very early age that "this is it" and so you keep going. I loved chasing down a story, the danger of a deadline closing in, the thrill of a scoop, the characters in the newsroom, and the contacts—leaders from all walks of life—I had the opportunity to meet and was privileged to get to know. And of course the generous newsroom mentors who made it possible for me, even though I was a cocky pain-in-the-neck in the early days—overcompensating for the fact that I was scared to death half the time working in a newsroom the size of a football field, with police radios buzzing static in one corner, people shouting at each other in another corner, and a thin blue haze of cigarette smoke hovering over those old Underwood typewriters.

But there was one moment that will always stand out. I was at my newspaper's Christmas party one year chatting casually with a newsroom veteran about all of this when I received a memorable piece of advice: "Don't love something that is incapable of loving you back." It was pure dumb luck that I left the newspaper business a decade ago to accept a job offer I couldn't turn down (at the PGA Tour), but I've certainly watched with sadness as journalism has broken the hearts of many since then.

This book wouldn't be complete without sharing some insights with you about where the news media business is today and what it's like for reporters whose careers today often feel like they are standing in the middle of a barely frozen lake on very thin ice, listening to the ominous sound of cracks all around them.

Let's start at the beginning. Journalists put the most thought and effort to the first paragraph of their story. It's known as the "lede" paragraph, deliberately spelled that way because back in the old days of hot metal typesetting it was necessary to avoid confusion between the metal lead and the first paragraph lede. Meant to entice the reader to plunge deeply into the story, great ledes are celebrated. Horrible ledes are joked about and ridiculed. Sometimes writers "bury the lede" by placing the most fascinating information at the end of a story. Sometimes the lede is just magical. You cannot help but read on. Here's an example of a great lede written by a young reporter, Claire Suddath, that sums up how journalists are feeling these days:

"Journalists are confused and scared. We work long hours for relatively unimpressive paychecks—the youngest of us scramble for unpaid internships, most of which don't even lead to full-time jobs—and we are working in an industry that's changing so fast that we have to hold panel discussions to figure out what the heck is going on. Print publications are bleeding subscribers, traditional nightly news programs can't figure out how to stay relevant, and even the brightest, most adaptable journalists have not yet learned how to get people to pay for their work. Basically, we're like the music industry, except none of us can sing."

It was the lede of a story about a panel discussion on the future of journalism held at Chicago Ideas Week and hosted by then-*TIME* magazine Managing Editor Richard Stengel (who subsequently went on to be named Under Secretary of State for Public Diplomacy, leaving *TIME* in winter 2014). Like all such panels—and there have been many—it was a sobering discussion. *TIME* has seen newsstand sales plummet 50 percent and has been forced to resort to multiple rounds of layoffs. There was also a former managing editor of the *Chicago Tribune* on hand, whose company had filed for bankruptcy. The other speakers were experts on digital, representing the leap the media business needs to make from its traditional news-gathering model to an online platform that generates revenue.

## Media Darwinism

Essentially the problem boils down to this: News media companies have not been able to adapt to the internet. As we discussed earlier, in the pre-internet era media outlets had captive audiences. It was common then for a story to "break" when copies of the newspaper were delivered early in the morning. Morning radio would "scalp" the story in abbreviated form on the news at the top and bottom of each hour and TV news assignment editors would send reporters out to do "matchers"—stories that would report this news item, or advance it, on the 6 and 11 P.M. evening news.

The subject of the story, and the subject's PR people, would scramble in the morning to plan how they would communicate a response to all the journalists who would be following up on the story. The 24 hours between that newspaper edition hitting someone's front porch in the morning, to the next day when the next edition landed, was known as the "24-hour news cycle."

Crisis communications managers focused on what they could do to improve news coverage by clarifying facts, updating information and getting spokespersons in front of TV cameras for the next 24-hour cycle. It's also why there are so many legendary stories about journalists and bars—few better than Pete Hamill's *A Drinking Life*—because once the newspaper or broadcast was "put to bed" there was a sort-of blackout period (both for news delivery and the alcohol-induced kind) until the next news cycle began.

That has all changed in the internet era. There is no such thing as a 24-hour news cycle. The news cycle is literally minute-by-minute.

Reporters, for the most part, don't hit the bars anymore; they hit the gym. They are never more than a short reach away from their smart phones. Traditional media outlets cannot "break news" any more—or very rarely—thanks to social media. A major newspaper can break a story based on its own investigative work, but chances are you won't hear about it from the actual newspaper. Instead you will see it posted on a social media site via a Twitter or Facebook feed to your smart phone. Studies show that about 50 percent of Facebook and Twitter users regularly re-post news stories.

The ability to access news online in real time has caused massive cancellations of print copies of newspapers—to the point where many believe print editions will soon be extinct. As eyeballs fled the hard-copy print newspapers and circulation plummeted, advertisers soon realized they were not reaching their audiences.

A stunning statistic: Total newspaper advertising revenue was down 49 percent in 2013, from a decade earlier.[1] Much of the classified advertising went to online sites like Craigslist or eBay. Display ads were sucked up by Google and Facebook, among others. That decline in newspaper advertising revenue is even more shocking to contemplate when you realize that media get about 70 percent of their total revenue from advertising.

Seemingly there is an easy solution: If everyone is getting their news online, newspapers just need to move their advertisers to their online sites, right? Not so fast. Click-through rates on online banner ads are extremely low. They average about 0.1 percent—meaning that for every 1,000 people who see an ad online, one person will click on it to read the ad content. Therefore, the return from online advertising is low. For every $1 newspapers gain in online advertising, they lose $7 in print revenue.[2] That's just an unsustainable business model.

It is also why newspaper staffing has fallen to levels not seen since the mid-1970s and continues to fall.[3] It's a struggle for survival. There is even a website dedicated to the topic: newspaperdeathwatch.com, that lists the U.S. metropolitan daily newspapers that have closed since 2007. Costs are being slashed. Some newspapers are actually cutting back on the number of days per year that they publish. Many newspapers large and small are forcing existing staff to take extra unpaid days off each year, to reduce payroll costs. And payrolls costs are already low. The U.S. Bureau of Labor statistics reported that in 2013, the average reporter salary was lower than the average U.S. salary for all jobs ($44,360 for reporters; $46,440 on average for all jobs).[4] There is no end in sight.

After much hesitation, newspapers are generally moving toward a pay wall model, even though reviews in terms of revenues are mixed at best. Most experienced internet users (and I say this as a multiple online newspaper subscriber who pays for access) know there are easy ways for users to circumvent those pay walls. All this has caused wave after wave of layoffs, not just at newspapers but all media outlets including TV, magazines, and radio.

Veteran journalists fall into two basic camps—

1) The firm holdouts who say, "You will get my job when you pry it out of my cold dead hands."

2) The realists who want to stay but agonize with each pending

buyout package whether they should take the offer now on the table rather than risking a straight layoff where the terms and the timing might not be to their advantage.

## Changing Media Priorities

So where does that leave you? In a much more precarious position when your crisis breaks than you would have been a decade ago. We've talked about speed and its dangers, but it really is true. For today's media it is far more important to be first than to be right. There has been much agonizing over this trend, but up against the competition from social media, traditional media outlets (some now refer to them as "legacy media") have no choice.

For today's media it is far more important to be first than to be right.

Two things are a certainty: When a crisis breaks you are less likely than ever before to be dealing with a veteran reporter, someone who knows about your company or your industry; and secondly, the reporters will spend less time with you gathering the information because they have so much more on their plate.

The reporter's first priority in many cases will be to tweet—not just right after interviewing you, but even before (*#onassignment In a cab headed to Company X to get to the bottom of this*). Different media outlets have laid out various policies for their reporters: to attract a certain number of Facebook or Twitter followers, or to put up a certain number of posts per day.

Print reporters are shooting videos at news scenes with their smart phones. TV reporters are recording voice-over stories for radio stations. As media ownership has consolidated, it is the young multi-tasking reporter who is surviving in journalism today, as opposed to the beat reporter who may have specialized in your business sector for a decade or more and was capable of bringing perspective and context to a breaking news story. As a result, it will be more incumbent upon you to provide that context and information and to get it out quickly.

The heartbreak for many journalists comes not just from the layoffs and ensuing loss of outstanding talent, but also from the dumbing-down of serious online news sites—with Justin Bieber and Kim Kardashian news, for example—in order to drive page views and boost advertising revenue.

It also comes from the increasing violation of basic principles of journalism that have held true for hundreds of years, since the advent of newspapers in the 17th century—namely the "separation of church and state" represented by the distinct division between editorial and advertising.

It has always been critical for the news media to protect its public integrity as an industry by strictly separating these two functions. The theory was that journalists could truly and independently defend the public interest because it was impossible for wealthy individuals or corporations to "buy" influence on a media outlet's coverage through the advertising channel. There has never been absolute purity in this regard, but by and large the principle held true.

Even that is rapidly changing.

The Pew Research Journalism Project's *State of the News Media 2014* report found that "the overlap between public relations and news noted in last year's State of the News Media report became even more pronounced." According to the report, "One of the greatest areas of revenue experimentation now involves website content that is paid for by commercial advertisers—but often written by journalists on staff—and placed on a news publishers' page in a way that sometimes makes it indistinguishable from a news story." The struggling *New York Times,* the *Washington Post* (which was saved when Amazon's Jeff Bezos purchased it for $250us million) and the *Wall Street Journal* have all begun to devote staff reporters to this kind of advertising, which they refer to as "custom content."[5]

Mainly, the practice is called "native advertising" because the ads are provided in a look and feel online that is consistent with actual news content the user sees. Proponents says it is "less intrusive" advertising, while opponents say it is worse (and far more offensive) than the traditional advertorial content; it is advertising pretending to be real news.

It's also happening on social media. Advertisers can now purchase posts on Facebook, Twitter, or Instagram. Even the venerable news media agency of record, the Associated Press, began in 2013 to allow sponsored tweets (from Samsung) onto its main Twitter feed.[6]

The survey firm eMarketer reported that native advertising spending reached $1.63 billion (U.S.) in 2012 and forecast that it would reach $2.85 billion by 2014.[7] That's too much money even for the purest of journalism's puritans to shrug off given the current state of the media business model. *Wall Street Journal* editor-in-chief Gerard Baker was reported by Pew Research to have expressed reservations, but reasoned that he is "confident our readers will appreciate what is sponsor-generated content and what is content from our global staff."[8] That may be wishful thinking.

There are some contrarians out there who predict big things for the future of journalism. One is software engineer Marc Andreessen, the co-founder of Netscape and the visionary who created Mosaic, the first popular web browser. The World Wide Web Hall of Fame member, who sits on the board of directors of Facebook, wrote a blog post for his venture capital firm Andreessen Horowitz in which he declared: "I am more bullish about the future of the news industry over the next 20 years than almost anyone I know. You are going to see it grow 10X to 100X from where it is today. That is my starting point for any discussion about the future of journalism."[9]

Normally that statement could be immediately flipped into the junk file, but the truth is that you just cannot ignore a visionary of Andreessen's stature. You might not like what the future he envisions looks like, but it was summed up by the headline of his post: *The Future of the News Business: A Monumental Twitter Stream All in One Place.*[10]

He argued that journalism is just a business that today is going through restructuring—from pre-2005 "oligarchies and monopolies" to post-2005 completely open system where anyone can create and distribute content. The other change, he said, is that newspapers don't just compete with other newspapers; they compete with TV news and cable and radio, whereas all those media forms once competed only with like media.

People who predict the demise of media are too focused on the fact that these dynamics are pushing prices down, Andreessen wrote. What we're all missing, he argues, is that there are many more people consuming media than ever before and those volumes will continue to increase in the years ahead. Just based on the number of smart phones registered he believes there will be a market of 5 billion news consumers in the world by 2020.

Granted, Andreessen said existing union agreements and pensions need to be vacated to move the media business forward—a point of view with which many would violently disagree. He also advocates removing what he called the "Chinese Wall" between reporters and the advertising side of the business, saying there are "intermediate points between 'holier than holy' and 'hopelessly corrupt' when it comes to editorial content. Maybe we are entering into a new golden age of journalism, and we just haven't recognized it yet."[11] Maybe.

The truth is, we're all still guessing. My take is that big, trusted, reputable mainstream media will remain dominant players for decades to come. The investments by new media thinkers like Bezos will help these legacy media adapt at a faster pace.

I don't put much stock in the rise of so-called "citizen journalism"—other than those paparazzi gotcha cell phone videos of some celebrity or politician being somewhere or doing something they're not supposed to be or do. They are now a fact of life. Citizen journalism, with all due respect to citizens, has already taken fatal hits to its credibility with the reporting of hoax deaths and other nonsense.

Besides, there isn't a citizen journalist in the world who will be able to regularly be the first to report breaking news on social media because there are now hundreds of millions of citizens doing it. It's a given in today's smart phone culture that when something big happens, everyone will know immediately. What the public craves is context and meaning behind an event. And they want that explanation from a credible source they can trust.

Look at it this way, if you have a rash on your arm, you can go into a chatroom on the internet and ask any number of "citizen doctors" for a diagnosis or treatment ideas. They will be more than happy to weigh in. Some will try to get you to click on a link that will spam you with health-related sales pitches, or worse yet, send a virus to your computer. But there is no shortage of them. The declines in Twitter's stock in Spring 2014—including an 18 percent drop the day the lockup on early investors expired—tells me people are getting tired of the garbage they sometimes encounter on the web. While they won't abandon it there will be a flight to quality on the internet that will serve the news media well.

What about dealing with journalists?

Acknowledging my own bias, I can tell you this. I know or have known about as many of them as anyone you will meet and I can tell you they are smart and perceptive. They are high achievers. They have to be because journalism schools produce more graduates than there are jobs to fill.

They are bright, inquisitive, and personable. Although there is a trend toward "point of view" journalism tailored to certain demographic audiences, such as Fox News, by and large journalists are fair-minded people. If you deal professionally with them, they will be professional with you.

They tend to mirror your behavior. If you treat them like the enemy, they will treat you like the enemy. If you run (and hide), they will run (and chase you down). If you cooperate, they will cooperate.

Journalists are not inherently incented to "burn" people. That is a myth. There is nothing to fear about working with a reporter. If you are interviewed by a journalist, he or she is looking for you to be one of their future contacts—to be a source. It's better for the journalist to develop the relationship with you than to burn you on one story.

It's better for the journalist to develop the relationship with you than to burn you on one story.

Those reporters don't last because eventually no one will speak to them and their bosses back in the newsroom get tired of constant complaints about their behavior.

Today's journalists are struggling with all the issues we've discussed in this chapter. They are people working in a troubled industry, with uncertain futures. But they are fundamentally good people.

There—I buried the lede.

## Notes

1. www.journalism.org/2014/03/26/the-revenue-picture-for-american-journalism-and-how-it-is-changing/

2. www.poynter.org/latest-news/mediawire/165288/pej-newspaper-are-losing-7-in-print-revenue-for-every-1-in-digital-gained/

3. www.pewresearch.org/fact-tank/2013/06/25/newspaper-newsrooms-suffer-large-staffing-decreases/

4. http://ajr.org/2014/05/05/reporter-salaries-compare-jobs/

5. www.journalism.org/2014/03/26/state-of-the-news-media-2014-overview

6. www.ap.org/Content/Press-Release/2013/AP-provides-sponsored-tweets-during-electronics-show

7. www.forbes.com/sites/theyec/2013/08/28/the-growing-impact-of-native-advertising-on-brand-marketing/2/

8. www.journalism.org/2014/03/26/state-of-the-news-media-2014-overview/

9. http://a16z.com/2014/02/25/future-of-news-business/

10. Ibid.

11. Ibid.

# Chapter 14

# The Forgotten Ones

To VIVIDLY IMAGINE the critical importance of stakeholder communications during a crisis, think about—Heaven forbid—that painful scenario of what you would do automatically during a personal crisis, for example, a sudden death in the family.

Once you got past the immediate shock and your own emotional reaction and then consoled loved ones who were physically with you, one of the first things you would consider is how to tell others. You would start with immediate family, those closest to you. It would be a telephone call, not a text or email, because you would consider that too impersonal, verging on offensive.

You would probably sit down with one or two loved ones you were with and make a short list of those people who were the most important to inform immediately. You might even divide up those calls between two or three of you who are the *de facto* heads of the family. You may decide how much you want to tell them, or how you should explain what happened (you might not have all the facts yet). You might discuss how these people on the short list of first calls are likely to react, who they are likely to call, and what they're likely to say to those people they call. Is anyone on your short list likely to overreact?

Once your small group had completed calls to this short list, or even as the calls were underway, you might compare notes with each other as to how people were reacting and what questions they were asking. You would learn from the early calls which pieces of information you needed to stress and how to console people. Realizing you had other tasks before you, arrangements and other things you needed to get done, you would likely then prioritize a second tier of people who needed to be informed: that person's closest friends, their workplace if applicable, your church, volunteer (sports, charities) organizations the person had commitments to, and any others who needed to be reached out to individually. Finally, you would consider how to tell everyone else—the largest group of people. For that you might consider a death notice in the local newspaper, although many others are now turning to social media to share the news and allow others to sign online pages of condolences.

It is these exact same prioritizations that should occur during a crisis involving your company or organization. The closest immediate family members are your executive team. The initial short list of calls would be senior employees and others tied to the organization, for example the board Chair. You would gather information about how people were reacting after informing the short list and you would realize that now is the time when the news could leak out quickly.

The secondary list for notification would start with your employees—think of them like you would members of your extended family—and then include people like major customers or suppliers, government officials, regulatory bodies—all those stakeholders we discussed in terms of the stakeholder mapping process in Chapter 5.

Then, in very short order, would be your mass communications—telling everyone else. You would do that through multiple channels, including a media statement, calls to key journalists you knew for a heads-up, a press conference or media briefing and social media posts. These would all come in extremely rapid sequence, but the sequence is important.

## Never Forget Employees

Regrettably, in too many actual crisis communications situations, employees are the forgotten ones. Extending the analogy above, they are very much like family in many behavioral ways. They can be your greatest champions. They will be the people you will rely on most in these difficult days ahead. But they are also the people who are capable of being the most hurt and alienated if they feel they weren't important enough for you to contact with major news.

If employees read about a crisis involving their company online, through the news media, or on social media, there is a very good chance they will view it as a "break in the faith" in terms of the relationship with the company. They will question how well the company is organized to handle the crisis, drawing negative conclusions. Feeling out of the loop, they will tend to fill what they perceive to be a vacuum with speculation, gossip, and distraction. They will vent some anger. They would likely have done this anyway, but learning about the company crisis through the media only magnifies their frustration.

Some could decide that if they were not important enough for you to inform, it's time for them to refresh and re-circulate their résumé. They certainly won't be rallying to the company's defense on- or offline. And these are the people you need the most to ensure that everything you are executing during the crisis is 100 percent, because you just cannot afford a second mistake when you're under the microscope. So why would you want to distract them? You need them feeling confident and proud of what your organization stands for.

For example, I have worked on many hospital crises. A hospital is a diverse group of people, from the top surgeons to the generally under-appreciated nursing staff, to other clinicians and support staff. You typically also have dedicated volunteers attached to the hospital's foundation who give their time and effort to various fundraising activities. It is always critical in a hospital crisis that everyone attached to the organization feels empowered. They need to feel like the hospital CEO and the senior executive team is on top of the situation and in control. Many of the best and brightest in hospitals have highly mobile skill sets. It's not difficult for them to pack up and move into another hospital or clinical setting. Great emergency room doctors, for example, are always in demand. So a crisis can be a time when you deepen your organization's bond with these special people; or it can be a time when they feel like the ties have been cut.

That's why employees need to be among the first to know. So why do we so often put last one of the first things we should be doing during a crisis? Some of it is just human nature. Let's face it, the two words "stakeholder relations" do not exactly form the most exciting title, one that is bound to stir emotions and compel action. When a crisis is on in your organization and people are running around talking about the crew from the TV station arriving, who is briefing the Board of Directors, how the press conference is going to be set up, who will be media training the CEO, who is managing your social media feeds—all fairly exciting stuff—it's easy to overlook your key stakeholders.

The best way not to overlook them is to make them part of your ongoing crisis communications preparedness. It's sometimes the case that you just cannot tell your employees of a crisis before they see it in the media—because you didn't know either. The media broke the story wide open. However, what helps reduce the second-guessing is that you've explained this to your employees in the past when you've discussed with them your organization's crisis communications planning process. They know what can happen and they know where to turn within their department or unit for more information. They can also expect that you will be communicating with them shortly, and when you do so, you validate their faith in the organization.

Remember too, that sometimes families of employees can lose their faith at a time of crisis. You need to be sure that if your employees don't have a way to communicate with their families, for example, if you are a school board and one of your schools is in lockdown, that you have a system in place to reassure families and provide up-to-date information.

All your employees should also understand their roles. From the people who answer the phones to the sales staff who are out meeting customers every day, your employees will get hit with questions about the crisis and they need to understand how to respond.

Even employees who are not external-facing in your organization will get asked by family and friends about the crisis, and what they say to those family and friends will likely get repeated to people in their social circles and so on:

*"Oh, my company is on top of it. We have trained and prepared for situations like this. We are proactive. There is a system that gets put in place to ensure safety at all times while we get to the root of the problem and the company will be quite open about that process."*

That's the kind of proud, confident answer you want your employees giving. As opposed to:

*"I don't know what the heck is going on. It seems to change every 5 minutes. I think they're in full-blown panic mode. We'll all probably lose our jobs. People must think we are a bunch of idiots. I am probably going to get screwed. So I don't really give a damn."*

It is always possible that employees who are feeling disenfranchised might decide to revolt against you, which is a very bad outcome during a crisis. That happened in 2013 at British music retailer HMV when it was in the process of laying off 190 employees at its head office and entering bankruptcy protection. A group of employees took over the U.K. company's Twitter account. The account has since been closed but an image of the page, widely shared online, shows the employees lashing out at HMV. It started with:

*We're tweeting live from HR where we're all being fired! Exciting!! #hmxXFactorFiring*

Next was:

*There are over 60 of us being fired at once! Mass execution, of loyal employees who live the brand. #hmvXFactorFiring*

Another that was massively re-tweeted was:

*Just overheard our Marketing Director (he's staying, folks) ask "How do I shut down Twitter?" #hmxXFactorFiring*

Within 30 minutes there were more than 1,300 re-tweets around the world and the story was picked up by major newspapers across North America (*USA Today,* Jan. 31, 2013) and Europe (*The Guardian,* Jan. 31, 2013). In other instances, disgruntled employees have attacked more surreptitiously, through what journalists often refer to as the "brown envelope," delivering an anonymous leak of damaging news. It's all, as we say, sautéed in the wrong sauce.

It is human nature for people to want to help. Your employees will feel frustrated if they think there is no way to contribute. So in your crisis planning and training, think about how people in various parts of your organization can contribute. To make that happen, work closely with your Human Resources lead, or if you are a small organization or company, with a human resources consultant who is teamed with your corporate communications lead.

Set up a system whereby crisis communications and protocols are part of the human resources-based training programs your company or organization requires all employees to participate in. Trust me on this: Employees won't push back. On the contrary, this is a very popular area for professional development, particularly with young employees. Having participated in countless training programs at various companies and organizations, I can tell you employees attend with excited antici-pation of crisis training—as opposed to, say, media training, which they approach like they would dental surgery—and they generally say how much they enjoyed it and would like to do more. (They say that about media training too, but only afterwards.)

A great time to do this kind of crisis training for employees is when you have a company retreat. When setting up working sessions, put one together on crisis communications and you will generally find it will be fully subscribed. The more your employees know about your company's policy and process around crisis, the less prone they will be to panic and second-guessing the day a crisis hits.

Remind them of the critical role they have to play during a crisis—every employee at every level of the company. They want to understand what they can do to help and what the proper channels of communication are within the organization. Providing them with this information in advance—and updating it on an ongoing basis—will reduce the sense of confusion within your offices and will tend to make your employees great ambassadors for your brand at a time of crisis.

## Leaks Happen Quickly

Here's the tricky part: Employee communications must always come before you speak to the media, but once you've told dozens, hundreds, or thousands of employees you need to get to the media fast. Why? Even the most thoroughly trained employees will find it difficult to keep information about the crisis bottled up. Things will begin to leak inadvertently—someone calls a spouse or a friend outside the organization—and it will happen far more rapidly than you think. You can ask for absolute confidentiality, but you cannot expect absolute confidentiality.

> You can ask for absolute confidentiality, but you cannot expect absolute confidentiality.

The best practice in this area is to be fully prepared for your media interaction in advance of meeting first with employees. Gather all your employees in one place if you can, or have the balance of your staff join by conference video, and once you've completed that meeting literally walk down the hall to the place where you will immediately begin speaking to the media, whether it be in a press conference, scrum, or series of one-on-one interviews. That's the order and it should be rapid-fire.

In this speed-of-light social media world we live in you cannot afford to have leaks coming out in a time lapse between your employee meeting and speaking to the media, that allow others to frame your story. You need to not only be the first to set that story frame, but to be well-established as the voice of authority in the crisis, one that people can turn to for regular updates and information.

You simply don't want to be in a reactive communications mode in a crisis. That goes without saying. You want to proactively set the message agenda with your employees, other stakeholders, the media, and the general public. We'll talk more about employee communications later on, when we discuss re-launching and re-engaging post-crisis.

Meanwhile, there are other key stakeholders to think about. Going back to the four-quadrant model from Chapter 5:

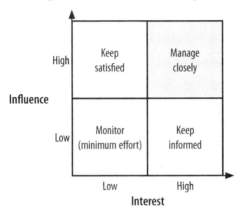

Your priority should be to communicate first with the stakeholders in the upper right quadrant, those who are both most supportive and most influential. All eyes tend to be on you, and on your sector, at a time of crisis and in the aftermath. If it is a transportation crisis in the airline industry or rail industry, that sector and its stakeholders will pay closer attention and will be sought out by media, government, and others for their point of view. The same is true of the education sector, the health care sector, the energy sector, or the financial services sector, and so on.

Your first job is to secure those who are already predisposed to support your organization and who have the influence to make a difference. They should be brought inside the tent and kept there.

The most influential of all should be on your CEO's call list—even a short call between media interviews will be surprising and impressive. That stakeholder will tend to feel like you are in control if your CEO has time to calmly and efficiently reach out by telephone to provide an update. It also impresses upon that stakeholder how important you feel he or she is.

So have the people in your organization consider in advance who those most important stakeholders would be. They should be on a call list, along with the names of stakeholders your CEO feels are important or with whom he or she has a particularly good relationship.

Remember, too, that when it comes to stakeholder calls there are the "must calls" like government officials and regulatory agencies, and then there are the "trust calls" to people who you trust and who you think can influence others. Some people are social influencers in a more powerful way than their title or resume might suggest. For example, the elected politician who heads your sector's federal or state/provincial department may be a must call, but often it is a member of the caucus who ultimately will be more influential, or even a backroom political organizer with a large network of contacts.

This is why we discussed earlier the need to coordinate your stakeholder assessment work with your government relations advisers. Similarly, you may have a long list of suppliers to your company, but your staff or CEO may recognize that there are two or three suppliers who are extremely influential within your sector and should be prioritized, regardless of the size of the business they do with your company.

It's not just that you want to think about stakeholders in your sector that the media could potentially reach out to, it's that you want to get to those people who will ultimately speak to the largest number of people about your crisis—and you want to arm them with the correct facts about what you are doing to make it right.

Don't forget, either, that sometimes stakeholders will surprise you at a time of crisis. So return your calls. A stakeholder might reach out to you—even a competitor—who wants to help out and support you at a time of crisis, but they certainly won't be able to do that very effectively if their calls or emails are not returned.

## Keep on Task

That's why it's acutely important to stay focused and eliminate any busy work you needn't be doing. Zoom in on the strategically important tasks you've discussed before in crisis preparedness discussions. As we've said, it's not a checklist, per se, but a process. And stakeholders are a hugely important part of that process before, during, and after a crisis.

There is another element to stakeholder communications that is essential at a time of crisis and that involves third-party, independent analysis. This is something you do when the initial stages of the crisis have been successfully dealt with and you are about to round the corner into a posture of recovery.

It's not enough, in every case, to tell the public that you are investigating and that you will do the right thing in terms of making the kinds of changes that will ensure the crisis doesn't happen again. This is particularly true in any crisis involving public safety. Your own internal investigation is absolutely essential, but it won't be given the same weight in terms of public opinion as an investigation by someone else who is independent of your organization.

Remember, if the public isn't satisfied that the risk has been drastically reduced, or eliminated, they will make that known to elected officials. In some crises, governments have been forced into launching public reviews (by committees, for example) or full-on public inquiries. These can be more unpredictable and sometimes colored by actions that are motivated primarily by political calculations, as opposed to just the facts surrounding the incident. Participants in politically appointed reviews, in other words, might take a certain hard line not because they think that is what your company deserves, but to make their political opponents look bad.

That's not to say that you should resist an inquiry ordered by a government. In fact, in every case your media statement in response to the announcement of a government review is that you welcome it and will cooperate fully. But there are ways to reduce the likelihood of that happening.

Let's assume you have instigated and shared your own internal review, what you learned and what steps you are taking as a result. That is table stakes. It must be done. But in a serious crisis you need to find independent experts who can conduct their own review and provide you with observations and recommendations that you will make public. This is an initiative you should share early on in the crisis process. The general public and your stakeholders will respond positively and you will have answers to potential media questions about whether your organization's own review is just self-serving and biased.

So, imagine a theoretical crisis in which you are a food manufacturer that sells products aimed at children. Through a mistake in your manufacturing process, your products marked "peanut-free" have had peanuts and other nut traces added, and several allergic children have gone into anaphylactic shock—in fact two have died.

You would, of course, do your internal investigation and fact-finding, but you would be well-served to, for example, appoint a three-member independent panel to conduct an investigation and report back. The panel could be comprised of a doctor or scientist recognized for work on food allergies involving children, a representative of an awareness organization (such as FARE, the Virginia-based national Food Allergy Research and Education, or Anaphylaxis Canada), and a retired or current senior official from the public health sector.

The makeup of this independent group is also something you can check in advance with a few respected stakeholders, including government officials. If you have already established an independent review conducted by the same kind of experts that the government would turn to, it vastly reduces the need for the government to fund a review that would essentially duplicate it. Your government stakeholders may have some valuable advice as to the makeup of the independent review or its methodology. Increasingly, cash-strapped governments are looking to industry sectors to lead in areas such as public safety. And it is always better in a crisis environment for you to be initiating and leading in terms of actions.

This is another example of shattering expectations—better to be seen to be initiating an independent review of what happened, than to be viewed as being forced into cooperating with a review that was dropped on you. It is consistent with the underlying theme of surprising people as to what an organization like yours would do at a time of crisis. It demonstrates leadership, transparency, and a commitment to getting it right.

Your senior team may feel that there is absolutely no chance that your internal review will miss any relevant aspects of what happened. But reality is perception. Going this extra step removes the perception of self-interest and helps cement your commitment to the public interest.

# Chapter 15

# Recovery

IN THE SURGICAL WARDS of hospitals there is a place typically referred to as the ICU (intensive care unit) where patients go after surgery, to be monitored, usually to be weaned off the most powerful pain medications, and to be stabilized before they are moved into a regular hospital bed down the hall. At this stage, the doctors think they made the right diagnosis and they believe they know what went wrong with the patient.

Opening someone up allows surgeons to see things, sometimes, that even MRIs cannot detect, so all the information on the patient is definitely in hand. And they've taken the surgical steps to repair what went wrong, hopefully, so it won't happen again—although there are never any guarantees.

Still, the patient is far from being ready to go home and resume his or her normal life. There is a long road ahead before that happens. But this is a turning point. It is in these hours and days that you learn whether the surgery was a success and the patient is on the road to a full recovery, or whether the problem is more serious than first believed and there is little else to be done: the patient is terminal. In the latter case, you can manage pain and prolong the patient's life, but that life will never be the same again.

There is a stage in a crisis where you and your organization are this patient. You are in the ICU. All the information has been gathered. The problem that caused your crisis has been diagnosed and steps have been taken to fix it.

You are not, by any means, ready to re-launch yet (for example, if you are a food manufacturer that recalled a product, you're not ready to put it back on store shelves). The situation needs to be monitored closely.

People will be taking readings on how well you managed the crisis, or how poorly you did. Inevitably, some will comment that you haven't done enough. Others will laud your actions and applaud your commitment to making things right. The big question for your organization at this stage is: Will you return to operations as they were before (or even better), or is your brand essentially terminal, or somewhere in between?

And just like a patient, this is where all your behavior in the years gone by takes on meaning for the outcome.

If you are the corporate equivalent of someone who sat around for the last 20 years eating extra-large pizzas, smoking two packs of cigarettes a day, and polishing off a 12-pack of beer each night, you will likely learn you have heart disease or worse. As an organization, your days will be numbered. Or maybe this crisis was the heart attack waiting to happen, and you are already finished as a brand.

But if your company worked hard, built meaningful stakeholder relationships, trained employees to understand crisis communications and protocols, executed an efficient and focused crisis communications plan, and, most importantly, brought a clear public interest focus to dealing with the issue, you will be like the pink-lunged jogger who exceeds the projected recovery time and is back in peak condition quickly.

If you shattered public expectations about how a company in your sector would behave in a crisis situation like this one, you could emerge as the corporate equivalent of the Bionic Woman, even stronger and more capable of great achievements ahead.

So is everything already decided for you at this stage of the crisis? Is there nothing more left for you to do? Not exactly.

## Small Steps

You still need to take your medicine. You still need to start to get out of bed and go for short walks down the hallway. It starts with those small steps. You are not rebuilding your health, you are rebuilding your credibility. You are stress-testing your brand with stakeholders. If some are angry or disappointed, you will need to address those concerns and mend those relationships. And of course you will need to reassure your family—your employees—that the organization is on the road to recovery and not to worry—things will be back to normal soon.

The first thing you need to do at this stage is to take stock. Sit with your senior team and ask yourself: How did our plan work? What is the current tone and volume of social media posts? How many media requests are we getting per day and what is the trend of the coverage? Do we need to re-map our stakeholders? Or did those relationships hold up as true and supportive? If they did, how can we thank those people? How is the mindset of our employees? How will we recognize their contributions to this crisis communications effort—particularly those who likely worked through long hours on nights and weekends to get the organization through it?

Critically, you need to ask yourself: Where are we with our fact-finding mission and external investigations, and what concrete steps have we taken? What did we promise in the heat of the crisis moment and are we living up to that today, or are we cutting corners now that the adrenaline has faded? This is a time to live up to all of your commitments, and then some.

Most importantly, this is the moment when you need to take a step back.

Stop running from task to task, like you have been during the crisis. Take some time to think. Talk to some people outside of your normal professional circles. Not people with informed opinions or reasons to flatter you, but "real" people.

Look at some data if you have the resources to survey public opinion, but in my view, time and resources are better spent doing a focus group. Have all your senior team sit behind the one-way glass. You have been so immersed in the crisis that it is now impossible for you to see things objectively. Before you take those first few tentative steps forward is the time you absolutely need clear, unbiased, objective feedback. As much as you love your team of employees and external consultants who've worked tirelessly at your side through the ordeal, they aren't capable of being objective either.

It's my very firm belief that one of the biggest mistakes we make at this stage of the crisis is failing to obtain that objective reading about where the public is, where consumers are. We are just too close to it. This can cause you to go down a path that could be a massive misreading of the situation. It's possible you've vastly over-estimated the extent to which people are still thinking about your crisis. But it's also distinctly possible that—due to the pride you may feel about how well your team executed—you've missed completely the visceral reaction people still have to you and your brand. This is the time to take stock, before you move forward. You cannot afford to stumble now.

"Recovery" is actually a separate stage in the crisis communications process.

Sometimes organizations forget that "recovery" is actually a separate stage in the crisis communications process. They do the corporate equivalent of jumping off the operating room table, heading out on the street and hailing a cab to the airport to the next business meeting. Not so fast.

You really do need to take stock before re-launching operations as normal. Once you've done that you can start to put together a re-launch communications and marketing strategy.

## Take Care of Employee Morale

But before you get there, you need to do something out of the ordinary for your employees. They also need to heal from this crisis experience. They need to feel like you as a leader, or the organization as an entity, appreciates what they went through, the efforts they put in during the crisis, and their loyalty in remaining to rebuild credibility.

Toyota provides a good example of this, having gone through recalls of millions of vehicles worldwide from 2009–2011 due to various issues, but primarily caused by unintended acceleration. Toyota kept its employees abreast of developments during the crisis using a Fast Facts internal email system that addressed key points.[1] These employee communications were sent before the media was made aware of breaking news.

But it was also important after the crisis to rally Toyota employees and dealers, certainly across North America where the brand had really taken a beating and been the subject of several lawsuits and investigations. Toyota management looked at ways to thank employees for pulling together at this difficult time and came up with a program called "Gestures of Appreciation" that involved fun events like large outdoor lunch gatherings with a DJ.

Eventually Toyota went further in terms of its re-launch strategy, as can be viewed on its press pages online.[2] This is where, in addition to news about Toyota brands and financials, you see stories about Toyota's work on fuel cell technologies, on environmental initiatives the company is taking, its support for the Wounded Warrior program, a program to support post-secondary education, as well as Toyota's latest social media posts. It's clearly a company moving forward, being a good corporate citizen, and building solid stakeholder relationships.

And there was proof that it worked. By 2013, Toyota outsold General Motors and Volkswagen to retake the global sales lead.[3] Toyota sales grew 23 percent to overtake the two other auto giants. The critical thing for Toyota to have prioritized, in my view, was addressing the issues of employee morale and making sure that staff felt appreciated. Those are the people who ultimately are responsible for Toyota quality and who drive Toyota sales. This was a time when Toyota needed to get it right and could not afford any missteps in terms of vehicle quality. Focusing on some reinvestments in their own people has paid off generously.

## Documentation

Some day, two or three years from the time of your crisis recovery— perhaps 10—someone from your organization will want to look back at exactly what happened and how you handled it. They will want to know things such as how quickly did call volumes increase and to what level? What did social media look like at various stages of the crisis? What do the notes say about stakeholder discussions during the crisis? And which messages worked well and which messages failed to gain traction? At what point did you take certain actions (product recall, press conference briefings, etc.) and how were they organized? How did your employees react initially?

Most importantly, beyond all the raw data, those people will want to know what your team's observations were about things that were executed well and things that could have been done better. It's while you are in this recovery phase, and the crisis is still fresh, that it's best to document the internal processes and observations good and bad. Much of the information will be at hand already, such as media logs, social media reports, call center logs, and minutes of your crisis team meetings. It's a matter of pulling it all together into one piece of documentation that adds valuable context.

Remember, everyone is learning as they go in the modern world of crisis communications so we owe it to each other to share these experiences, certainly within our own organizations. It's also worth noting that in crises that lead to legal action, much of this timeline and detail will be required by your lawyers. It may also be requested by regulatory agencies. And in some cases, those studying crisis communications at the university level will want to do case studies—for example several have been done about the successful crisis communications approach of Maple Leaf Foods during the Listeriosis crisis in Canada during which 22 people died from infections caused by the bacteria.

What works best in preparing such documentation is debriefing individual members of your team. This should be done through your HR department and should involve people at all levels of your organization in order to gather various perspectives. People should be able to share their views anonymously. Some will vent. For some, that venting will bring closure.

Ultimately, what you are doing at this recovery stage is adjusting your strategic viewpoint and tactical imperatives from the immediate term to the long-term view. During the crisis your focus was on immediate issues and rapid decision-making. Now you are about to pivot to a different stance. What has this crisis meant to your employees? How has it redefined your company (positively or negatively) to stakeholders and the general public?

Remember, Toyota's responses to its recall crises of 2009–2011 were widely criticized initially. But the company had enough brand equity to regain its stature once it started executing more effectively and put a longer-term strategic plan in place.

It's important as you assess what just happened to your organization to look at what actions you took that you are proud of and that you think define your brand. Think about actions or decisions that didn't meet that mark. Ultimately, what you want to do now is express that definition of your brand to your employees, stakeholders, and the public. Is your focus now squarely on safety? Are you more open and engaged as an organization? What are you saying about the importance of your customers, particularly those customers who remained loyal to you throughout the crisis?

We're not talking about re-branding your company entirely, but we are talking about updating and adjusting your brand to reflect its values—values that you demonstrated or wanted to demonstrate during the crisis.

Now is the time for you to continue to be real with people. Hopefully your crisis response was authentic and focused on the public interest. How can you extend that? If you earned good will for your crisis response, how can you continue to earn that good will by being a responsible corporate citizen and contributor to your community or communities? What would your employees be motivated to see you do in this regard? What would engage them and increase their loyalty to your organization? These are all the questions that you need to begin asking.

If you've largely failed at managing your crisis, of course you won't be trying to build on what happened, but rather you will need to consider starting from scratch. For some organizations that have had disastrous crises, complete brand re-launch has been the best option available to them.

One of the things you will find about yourself after the crisis is that if you didn't fully appreciate all that time you had during normal operations as an opportunity to prepare for a future crisis, you certainly will now.

So as a result, this "taking stock" process will almost certainly lead to you and your team wanting to put a more robust ongoing crisis communications training and issues management process in place. It may be that your weakness was stakeholder relations and you now realize that is an area where you need far more focus. It may be that you dropped the ball on employee communications—an increasingly critical area—and you need a more comprehensive internal communications program put in place.

These are normal outcomes of experiencing a crisis. Depending on the extent to which you used external consultants and experts during the crisis, you might want to bring in a different external expert now to review both the documentation of your crisis that you have compiled and these other policies that you now intend to update. It always helps to have that additional outside perspective. It could be that an external crisis expert might have additional ideas and value to add in terms of what you can be doing to move forward.

Any of us who have been through a personal crisis, be it a medical one leading to surgery as we've talked about in this chapter, or a sudden and tragic death in the family, go through certain stages in terms of our reactions.

But a time comes after arrangements have been made, after the sermon and the funeral, after the wake and all the thank you cards have been mailed out, when we are alone with our thoughts again. For many, it's a time to reflect on their own life. People ask themselves, in direct response to the tragedy they've just endured: "Am I the person I want to be? Am I doing all the things I wanted to do? Do my family and friends, and also my colleagues at work and in the community, see me as the person I want them to see me as?" This is normal.

So I cannot urge you strongly enough to do one more thing before you leave the recovery phase—hold a retreat.

Pull your team together away from the office for at least a day. You don't necessarily have to have every single employee in the organization, but try to ensure that all business units and all levels of staff are represented. Make it for at a full day—ideally with an overnight so you can do something fun and social in the evening, then wrap up the next morning with a breakfast. Seize smart phones at the door—just force people to surrender them!

Don't miss the opportunity at this point in time to do something that you will never be in a better position to do: Imagine who you want to be as an organization. Coming out of a crisis, you'll be in a better position to do this because you will never have so much fresh data and feedback about your brand at your fingertips.

This is what many crisis advisers mean when they say "never let a crisis go to waste." Rahm Emanuel, the Chicago mayor and former White House chief of staff to President Barack Obama, has repeatedly been quoted as saying he believes you should, ". . . never let a good crisis go to waste when it's an opportunity to do things you had never considered or you didn't think were possible." (foxnews.com, Jan.11, 2011) Now is that time.

We talked about the need to shift your thinking now from the immediate-term to the longer-term view of your strategic objectives. To signal that prior to the retreat, give attendees something thought-provoking to read such as Harvard Business School professor Youngme Moon's outstanding book *Different: Escaping the Competitive Herd* (Crown Business, 2011). You want people thinking creatively at this meeting. Moon argues that when you have an opportunity to re-imagine your brand, you need to shatter expectations people may have of you. Sound familiar? She states: "Differentiation is a way of thinking. It's a mindset. It's a commitment. A commitment to engage with people—not in a manner to which they are merely unaccustomed, but in a manner that they will value, respect, and yes, perhaps even celebrate."[4] You might want to bring in a brand guru like Ted Matthews of Instinct Brand Equity, who splits his time between Toronto and Arizona, to run an exercise for part of the day to stimulate your group's thinking.

Coming into the retreat, you will have information about how your customers, employees, and stakeholders identify with your brand now, after the crisis. Coming out of the retreat you want to have some agreement on a bold, new way those people will identify more strongly and positively with your brand in the future.

## Notes

1. www.simply-communicate.com/case-studies/company-profile/how-toyota-executes-well-driven-strategy-recover-crisis
2. http://pressroom.toyota.com
3. /www.bloomberg.com/news/2013-01-28/toyota-takes-global-auto-sales-lead-from-gm-on-disaster-recovery.html
4. www.linkedin.com/today/post/article/20140324153640-2760389-re-imagining-personal-brand

# Chapter 16

# Re-launch

EVERYBODY loves a comeback story. Many have tried to assess why we love them so much. Perhaps it's because all of us, at some point in our lives, have failed at something and we know how hard it is to overcome that failure. In retrospect, we reason that the task seemed too difficult, or we didn't try hard enough, or we gave up too soon. Maybe we took shortcuts, didn't prepare for what life could throw at us, and were caught flat-footed.

Or possibly, there was no way to succeed—the failure could have been based on a set of unfair circumstances, or a random, tragic event such as an accident that derailed you from your dream. All we are left with are the what-ifs.

So when we watch someone, in a real-life news story or in a fictionalized movie based on a true story, who won't give up and who risks everything to realize their dream, it can be a very emotional experience. We can relate to it personally. It also cuts both ways: We can deeply admire someone for a courageous achievement; or we can loathe someone for how absolutely evil they are.

That's why a crisis, a failure, or a tragedy, humanizes even the most enormous organizations. When people think of Enron, they don't think of some hollowed-out glass tower in Houston, they think of the type of corporate greed and scandal epitomized by human characters they've known, real or fictional. People familiar with Enron would remember the real leaders behind one of the biggest corporate scandals in history,

Kenneth Lay and Jeffrey Skilling—but for most people, when they hear "Enron" they imagine the stereotype of the greedy corporate titan, like the Jordan Belfort character played by Leonardo DiCaprio in the movie *The Wolf of Wall Street*.

Typically, we want to see the comeback story succeed—we cheer it on. The public will celebrate your brand's perseverance when you re-launch, if you give them reason to.

One of the films that consistently ranks on the list of the American Film Institute's most inspiring movies of the last century is *Rudy*, the (mostly) true story of a Notre Dame football walk-on who didn't follow his expected path to a dreary steel mill job with his dad and brothers, but chased a dream (that everyone in his life considered crazy) of playing for his beloved Fighting Irish despite not having the physical size, the grades, or the financial means to do so.

## Coming Back

Comeback stories extend far beyond sports to people who have overcome disease and other health afflictions, or who just hung in there when life dealt them a nasty set of cards. Some of the stories that I really find highly motivating involve the latter—people who, through no fault of their own, must overcome horrible circumstances. Rather than give in to long odds and self-pity, they persevere.

One example is that of a young woman named Dawn Loggins. She struggled through Burns High School in Lawndale, North Carolina, living in poverty with her mother and stepfather, who both reportedly battled drug addiction. Often evicted, they moved from place to place. When both her parents lost their jobs, she lived on noodles. When the power was shut off, she did her schoolwork by candlelight. When the public utility turned off the water, Dawn and her younger brother Shane would walk 20 blocks to a local park to fill containers so they could drink and also shower or flush the toilet.

She was bullied for wearing the same dress to school, day after day.

Then, the summer before her senior year, the straight-A student attended an elite academic camp in Raleigh sponsored by the governor. When she returned home weeks later, her mother and stepfather were gone—vanished. They'd abandoned her and moved to Tennessee. By the time she tracked them down, their phone service had already been cut off.

Dawn was homeless, entering her pivotal senior year of high school. Various friends gave her couches to sleep on for a few weeks at a time. To make enough money to survive, she worked as a janitor at her high school in the mornings from 6 A.M. to 7:40 A.M., cleaning toilets and scrubbing floors, before her fellow classmates arrived. She was determined to keep her grades up.

Eventually the local school bus driver opened up her home to Dawn. The full-time janitors at the high school washed Dawn's clothes for her. Another student's mother helped Dawn fill out her college applications and urged her to "shoot for the stars," so she did.

Months later, when a response letter arrived from Harvard University, the family hosting Dawn left it out on the table and prepared to console her when she opened it and received the bad news. But she opened it to find an acceptance letter—with scholarship, to become part of the Harvard class of 2016.[1]

Against all odds, Dawn became the first person in her school's history to be accepted to Harvard, where she is now studying sciences, working part-time and planning some day soon to start a non-profit focused on helping other young people who face the same challenges she did. "From Homeless to Harvard" blared the media headlines. Remarkable.

No matter how bad your crisis was, no matter how badly beaten up you were in the press and on social media, no matter how far your sales have plummeted or your stakeholders have turned against you, now is the time to motivate your employees and fashion your own against-all-odds comeback story. It may require the grit of Secretariat, the determination of Rudy, and the will to succeed of someone like Dawn Loggins, but you can get there.

People want you to get there. Unless you fall into the distinctly "evil" category (like Enron, or Bernie Madoff), people will, generally speaking, welcome your comeback story. In Canada, Maple Leaf Foods' comeback from a truly horrific crisis was celebrated. People praised the Toronto-based company's values, specifically the leadership demonstrated by CEO Michael McCain. Part of the company's re-launch involved the announcement of an independent Food Safety Advisory Council and a Chief Food Safety Officer. The company also launched an online site called The Dish to keep consumers abreast of the latest developments in food safety and healthy eating.

People wanted to see Maple Leaf Foods succeed in its comeback, partly because they believed in the company's strong reputation and its leadership. There is nothing particularly different about the food Maple Leaf manufactures, beyond a greater commitment to safety. But it was the reputation and trust in the company itself that brought many consumers back. They now trust that Maple Leaf is thinking about feeding their families and wants to ensure quality and safety of their products served at the family dinner table. This was part of the branding effort in Maple Leaf's re-launch.

What we're learning is that, yes, people expect products to work as advertised, they expect services like airlines and cruise lines to deliver them to where they want to be, but even more importantly, people want to know about the company.

Near universal access to Google and other search engines like Bing in the developed world mean that consumers don't need to just find out about a company's product and its cost. They can find out how other consumers have reviewed the product. They can learn about how employees were treated by that company.

Many vacation websites like Travelocity provide extensive consumer reviews and ratings of hotels, airlines, restaurants, and attractions. People can also research online about any company's culture and about the people who lead the organization. If there is a physical location, they can check out Google street view to see what the neighborhood looks like. It all adds up to: What does this company stand for? What is its personality and what are its values?

In fact, the Reputation Institute's 2013 Leaders Survey polled 300 executives at many of the world's largest companies and discovered that 79 percent agreed that we now have a "reputation economy" in which who you are matters more than what product you produce.[2]

For example, what I hear people saying about American automakers like Ford and GM are not comments about specific models of cars, but that the American companies are working harder now following their bankruptcy filings to make better quality cars and it shows. People believe it.

And yet only 20 percent of those corporate leaders surveyed said they felt their own company was prepared to compete in this type of reputation economy. The survey found that 54 percent of the executives said their companies lacked a structured process for managing reputation; 45 percent said they were unable to leverage internal knowledge of stakeholder groups; and 34 percent said silos within their companies prevented necessary collaboration.

When you start to build your re-launch plan remember that it is not just about getting back to business. Don't just think about how you will market Widget A or other products. That's missing the big picture. You need to think about a re-launch that goes back to the basics by doing three things: Acknowledge what you've been through, tell people who you are and what you stand for, and explain your commitment to them now and in the future.

What is that commitment? How do you communicate it?

Hopefully the recovery process you've gone through has helped you and your team to arrive at certain insights about your organization coming out of the crisis. It's almost like therapy. You've learned about yourself as an organization. You've gone through the early stages of a creative process designed to brainstorm about who you want to be and now you need to make that happen.

Engaging a branding firm or working with an advertising agency on creative is helpful. But don't do that in a silo. If you bring in creative people who were not there with you during the crisis, and didn't experience what you did, just be aware that they may fall in love with a creative idea and push you toward a campaign that completely misses the mark in terms of re-launching out of a crisis. And they can be very persuasive—they are very talented advertising people after all.

So don't break up your core crisis team at this stage and slide back into silos. Keep that crisis team working together on this re-launch because the job is not done yet.

Be absolutely unbendable on one issue in terms of the re-launch plan. Be sure that what is being produced is one single plan, delivered in one single document. Don't have one marketing plan document here, another social media document there, a media relations plan over there, way over there an internal employee communications plan, in the middle a CEO executive profile plan, and up there a stakeholder plan.

Don't schedule a meeting where the agenda is those separate plans to be discussed as agenda items #1 through #6. You need your marketing team working with your corporate communications team and your HR group—everyone together—to design one integrated re-launch blueprint to be signed off on by your CEO. And they should all be working off the one theme, the one simple "discovery" about your brand that came out of the recovery process. When brainstorms get too carried away and off topic, make sure you have a designated "Brand Cop" in the room who will bring people back in line with what the data and insights from this crisis have told you. Then it becomes about fitting the pieces of the puzzle together and sequencing them.

I would be stabbing the table with my index finger if I were there with you right now to emphasize one key point about this overall plan: simplify, simplify, simplify.

When you think you've done heroic work simplifying your plan—simplify it by another 50 percent. Trust me.

As French poet and aviator Antoine de Saint-Exupéry famously said: "Perfection is achieved, not when there is nothing more to add, but when there is nothing left to take away."

A guy who has had a little bit (wink) of global success in marketing, Richard Branson, once said: "Complexity is your enemy. Any fool can make something complicated. It is hard to make something simple."

Kathryn Aragon, a Texas-based veteran copywriter and marketing consultant to brands around the world, says marketing ideas are too often way too complicated. And if you find the marketing concept as complex as the organization communicating it, there is very little chance that your audience will get it. Aragon argues, "The best message is based on one idea, well expressed. It's targeted to one person, appealing to one emotion, asking for one action to be taken."[3]

I would just add this: Think visually. Visuals are far more powerful than words, as we all know. And, whether we think it is a good thing or a bad thing, there is a massive shift underway that is seeing consumers of information move away from words and toward visuals.

A 2013 analysis showed that social media users on the main platforms share more than 5,000 images every single second of every day. The fastest-growing social media platforms, particularly among the coveted younger demographic, are image-based, including Instagram, Tumblr, and Pinterest.[4]

> Visuals are far more powerful than words; social media users on the main platforms share more than 5,000 images every second of every day.

The *Columbia Journalism Review* reflected the trend in Spring 2014 with its report that 9 out of 10 people age 18 to 29 watch online video and of that group, 48 percent get their news from online video.[5] The truth is—frighteningly in my view—for the most part, young people today just don't read. Maybe in this era of lightning-fast download speeds and myriad mobile phone apps they just don't have the patience for it.

It's not even a new phenomenon. The *New York Times* proclaimed "The Death of Reading" in a headline back in 1991. I know some very bright, award-winning university students who don't read anything—

and by that I mean, absolutely nothing they're not forced to read. Nada.

Consider this: Sweden's Royal Institute of Technology does a great program every year for its Masters of Science in Media Technology. In its eleventh year, the 2013 theme was "the future of news." The main project was titled *The Morticians (Death of Reading)* and here is the project description: "We are proposing the complete Death of Reading. The alphabet will be replaced by video, audio, pictures, and other modes of sensual perception. Based on the current developments and spotted trends, we believe that in the future all news will be consumed via audio and visual input. We go even further and claim that the quality of news will not decrease. We rather see a chance to achieve a higher quality with erasing the middleman of a story (news editor) and providing audio/video material directly from where the story happened, almost like an eyewitness."[6]

While no doubt there are many ex-newspaper hacks like me who are enticed by the notion of erasing news editors, all joking aside, this notion is both alarming and extremely difficult to argue against based on current trends. This is why, for example, that info-graphics have skyrocketed in popularity—they are visual.

Now before we write off words altogether, remember that visuals are not just visuals, but words can be visuals too. They are known as so-called "word pictures," simple sentences that place an image in the person's mind. A great book that I have frequently sent to clients in Canada and the United States is *Made to Stick: Why Some Ideas Survive and Others Die* by brothers Chip and Dan Heath. It is from 2007 and I think it still delivers value today, not just in terms of simplicity but how ideas can fire people's curiosity and make them want to know more.

It's also critical to never lose the human element at re-launch. Your psyche may say back to business as usual, but your employees might not be over it yet and your customers are likely to balk if you just blithely pick up where you left off as if nothing happened.

We talked about how a crisis humanizes an organization to a degree. We've also talked about the need for your initial crisis response to be human and authentic, not robotic and bureaucratic. The same holds true now at re-launch.

Your employees, your suppliers, customers, and your stakeholders have been through a difficult time with you. Social media has catalogued every moment of it. The mainstream media is watching to see your next move. So acknowledge the crisis and what it was like. Get your CEO out to talk to media to tell the story from end-to-end.

People love to hear about these issues in story form—a beginning, a middle, and an ending. It helps your organization to talk about how, at every stage, your No. 1 priority was the public interest. Now is the time, with the immediate danger over, the facts and remedial actions explained and the victims cared for, to talk frankly about how difficult it was.

You are setting the "story frame" for your comeback. In your communications plan you need to describe your intentions and put out some measurable markers in terms of where you want to be.

Re-launch plans are as different as sectors in our economy and the myriad types of crises that can occur. They also vary by the amounts of brand equity organizations held going into the crisis. But there are some basic things your re-launch plan absolutely needs to do. You need to once again acknowledge to consumers that you let them down; that you broke the promise your brand made to them to get them somewhere, to protect them from something or to safely provide them a good or service.

You may feel like you have done this countless times before, but you cannot talk about re-launch without going back to this acknowledgment. You need them to understand that you know, to some extent, how they felt, and that you have listened and will continue to listen to them. Next, you need to explain to people that you understand what you need to do—you need to regain their trust.

So when you are putting your integrated marketing-PR re-launch plan together you need to continue to think about the public interest. Put yourself in the mind of that person in the target audience you want to reach. Think about what some of those people behind the one-way glass said at the focus groups you conducted.

If you could look one member of your target audience in the eye, face-to-face, and say one sentence, what would it be? That is the foundation of your re-launch.

Now, in every way you communicate with them from paid media, to earned media, to a major speech by your CEO, to social media posts, to meetings with stakeholders and internal employee communications, you need to play back to people how they are feeling—prove to them that you get it.

The most fatal error in a re-launch post-crisis is the mistake of pretending it never happened; or of revisionist history that attempts to minimize the crisis. That will simply reinforce people's expectations of the way you would be thinking and acting—you will be validating their negative bias.

But if you shatter that expectation by continuing to demonstrate remorse and by acknowledging that you have work to do to regain their trust, you will have moved your organization forward.

## Notes

1. www.dawnloggins.org/about
2. www.reputationinstitute.com/thought-leadership/white-papers
3. www.kathrynaragon.com/secret-to-powerful-marketing/
4. www.forbes.com/sites/onmarketing/2013/07/02/the-shift-from-words-to-pictures-and-implications-for-digital-marketers/
5. www.cjr.org/news_literacy/kids_these_days.php?page=all
6. http://futureofmedia.se/news/group-project/the-morticians-death-of-reading/

# Chapter 17

# Reputation: The New Benchmark

IT HAS BECOME fashionable to talk about the sudden emergence of reputation management on the internet. But the truth is that the importance of reputation has been recognized at least as far back as the ancient Greeks. Socrates said: "The way to gain a good reputation is to endeavor to be what you desire to appear."

Today, there are those who will tell you (and sell you) that reputation management is all about SEO—search engine optimization on the web. They will tell you that reputation management is all about pushing down negative web results attached to your own name or your company's name. It's all about the internet.

That's like saying "my PR guy can spin us out of this crisis." I completely disagree. The premise of trying to control search engine results to shape your reputation is based on an entirely false premise, which is that your reputation is defined by the internet.

This is not to suggest that companies that offer to help control what people say about you on the internet are all scam artists—there are reputable companies out there that can protect you from some of the abuse the web has to offer. I agree that search engine results will always be part of a company's reputation. Just not the biggest part.

We've arrived at the point where, for most of us, when we see a really over-the-top negative web post about a company we immediately discount it. We think the company's competitor is up to something. Or if it's personal, our minds usually go to what kind of conflict happened there and why one party has decided to use the internet as a weapon. We see it as fairly limited in terms of being informative or even true.

Monitoring what people say about you online serves as a sort-of alarm system, an early warning sign of systematic problems your company may have, as we discussed in Chapter 7. You should be listening closely and responding with an ongoing issues management program that deals with these small problems with customers or stakeholders before they become big problems.

But your overall reputation will not be shaped by the internet, ultimately. It's just an open content platform and it isn't designed to be controlled, at least until or unless governments step in to regulate it. The fact that it is uncontrolled is both its charm and its limitation.

Eva Wiseman, a columnist and editor at the *Observer* in London (the magazine of *The Guardian* newspaper), wrote that as time goes on, we will "trust less" as we consume information on the internet because so often what is purported to be true is proven to be a hoax.

"And if this continues to happen—if it repeatedly reports on fictions as if they're fact—then won't it start to lose us, its fast-clicking readers?" she asked. "We don't expect every story posted by a stranger on Twitter to be true, but we do expect every story reported on by a huge media organization to be, because that's what they're for. The point of them is to filter through the daily mess of culture and to repackage it for us in witty, bite-sized, trustworthy chunks. The more they mess up, the less we'll return."[1]

Many have proclaimed that "the internet is a garbage dump."[2] The irony is, that story was on the internet, so we're not sure whether to trust it—but hold on, it is from *PC Magazine*, a trusted voice in the tech sector media, so okay. This is the calculation we must make every time we encounter information online. Is this credible?

Others have debated whether the internet is actually a garbage dump or an information feast. My answer is: both. You cannot discount the internet because there is a wealth of information and utility there. Who would have thought we could deposit checks in our bank account by taking a picture of them with our cell phones? It is the dominant platform today, by far, until the next one is developed. But in terms of it controlling and shaping your reputation, you can never count on it. There is just too much spam, garbage, and other automated nonsense available online that make it possible for anyone to do just about anything to anyone else that, on balance, it cannot be considered completely credible.

*TIME* magazine reported on a survey by the very credible firm Harris Interactive that showed 98 percent of us distrust what we see on the internet.[3]

As a result, many are predicting that the era of "blind faith" in the veracity of internet content is rapidly coming to a close.[4]

That is perhaps a good thing because my biggest concern is that organizations can become too obsessed with the minutiae of this one area of reputation management—not to be ignored of course, but put it in context—to the exclusion of far more critical determinants of one's reputation.

You can artificially push down negative comments about your company on the web, but if the interactions between customers and your brand continue to be negative there won't be a rock big enough to hide under. It will be like sticking bubble gum in the cracks of a dam to keep the water from bursting through.

Organizations and companies don't ultimately decide what these social media conversations will be like, despite what some digital strategists will tell you—people decide.

One of the new marketing trends that troubles me is so-called "viral marketing" where the company advertising sets out to determine what content people will fall in love with and share with others online, mimicking the true viral nature of some YouTube videos, for example. It's a great idea in theory and is cheaper than traditional advertising in terms of reaching a larger audience. But it is essentially fake.

Some of it is extremely well done, like the Pepsi Max YouTube video of NASCAR driver Jeff Gordon taking a test drive at a car dealership.

But that's just good advertising. There have always been great ads. To me, if the content is deliberately placed, it is by definition not "viral" because it didn't start with one individual and spontaneously spread to millions. It was placed there for that purpose, designed for a mass audience, and was likely pushed out in paid social media posts and other paid advertising means.

Just as there is no PR "silver bullet" to solve a crisis—it requires your organization to do the right thing—there is no reputation management silver bullet by trying to control internet content. Your reputation will be tested every time a customer interacts with you, testing your brand promise and hoping it will be true.

Did they take care of my luggage during the flight? Did that person at the other end of the help line actually help? Was this new tech gadget as easy to get up and running as they promised me it would be? This customer experience is below the radar of an actual crisis. But after you have emerged from a crisis, recovered, and re-launched, these are the reputational issues that can make or break your organization.

Now, the test is, "Are they living up to their promises?" Coming out of your crisis you've told people how you will behave, you've made statements about your standards and beliefs. So people will test you. They will only cheer your comeback if they feel that it is actually real, that you have turned over a new leaf. That's why you need to rally every single person in your organization to create your own come-from-behind story, to demonstrate grit, determination, and courage to get it right.

Actually being a better brand, and sharing what you are doing to be a better brand, is the fundamental principle of reputation today, not using algorithms to push down negative web results.

Just as you cannot hide a lie forever (see Lance Armstrong), the truth about how you are living up to your brand promise after a post-crisis re-launch will always "out" itself. That is the one undeniable truth.

When someone has a terrible experience with a company's help phone line, they'll still tweet about it. The people who follow that person's tweets will respond or re-tweet the information to their followers because they trust the source of the information. The same one-on-one interactions impact your organization's reputation when it comes to dealing with stakeholders, with suppliers, and with employees.

But this doesn't happen exclusively online. We all tend to ask someone whose judgment or experience we respect for their opinion about a company or service we are thinking of engaging. We might ask them through an email or a text message, so in that sense the communication is internet-based. But the trusted source of the information is key.

If you do check reviews of hotels on sites like Travelocity, as we've discussed before, they are of limited value because a) as we learned from *TIME*, 98 per cent of us don't trust what we read on the internet and b) there is such a wide range of opinions from extremely negative to extremely positive that you soon realize no hotel can be either that horrible or that spectacular. So you end up asking someone you know.

Bottom line? Reputation management is the No. 1 determinant of both your company's ongoing success and your ability to survive a future crisis, but it is not just about web results, it's about how you actually perform. At global PR firm FleishmanHillard they define the issue: "Reputation is a fundamental quality of every organization—what stakeholders believe about it, expect from it and say about it to others."[5]

What I want to stress—and what I hope is your key takeaway from this book—is that reputation is determined by what people expect of your organization. For you to thrive and survive after your crisis, people should now have a different expectation of what you will offer and how you will behave than they had in the past.

The British office of the Reputation Institute looked at the debate between those who would argue that: a) it doesn't matter what your reputation is, just how good your products and service are; versus b) the reality that "reputation . . . focuses on what people expect from a company . . . such as open and honest communication, playing an active role in society on issues that matter to people, leadership and governance, and strong performance."[6]

The group's survey found that 69 percent of people's willingness to say something positive about a company was based on their overall perception of the company, while just 31 percent said it would be based on what they think of the company's products or services.[7]

If you didn't realize this going into your crisis, hopefully you discovered it as you were making decisions about what actions to take to deal with the crisis. Prior to the crisis people had an expectation of how you would behave, much of it based on the public opinion conditioning we discussed in Chapter 2. Now you know how people have responded to your crisis actions. Now you have set out a re-launch plan that clearly sets out what you want people's expectations of you to be going forward. Think of it as a reputational road map.

I would argue it shouldn't be too difficult to exceed expectations in a positive way. In this cynical era we live in, a time when people are increasingly disengaged from pubic service and community activism, the bar is set pretty low. Many public expectations are negative ones.

So if you reinforce an expectation, for example, of being prone to dodging questions and withholding information, you will invite a more rapid and voluminous feeding frenzy of negativity during your crisis. But if you've correctly shattered expectations—truly surprised people with openness and transparency, or an amazing gesture and a positive action, that is when your reputation will grow.

As the Reputation Institute points out: "Business success depends on people supporting a company. That means customers buying products, investors buying stocks, regulators giving license to operate and employees delivering on strategy. For people to do this, they want to know that they can trust the company and it will live up to its promises."[8] The world has gotten smaller. We travel greater distances, more regularly, than ever before. We consume more information about other cultures. Even space travel has largely been demystified.

Companies are no longer just some obscure corporate entities that exist somewhere else. They have personalities. We treat our engagements with them—from the company that makes your laptop to the company that manufactures the car you drive—like we treat relationships. There are promises that need to be fulfilled, or we feel betrayed.

So understand that your reputation matters. You cannot SEO or advertise your way through it, no more than the bubble gum will prevent the flood from coming.

Having a program in place to work on it, year-round, is no longer a luxury. Given the dizzying speed and perilous twists and turns of the crisis communications world today, it is an absolute necessity.

So too is the need for everyone, from the CEO on down, to understand the crisis environment and our own instinctive tendencies when under attack. By recognizing and accounting for external conditions and our own internal thought processes, you will already be miles ahead in terms of making an initial positive step.

Even if you are blessed with never experiencing a crisis—which is extremely unlikely—a reputation management program will drive customer loyalty, motivate your employees, strengthen stakeholder relationships and, I believe, deliver to your bottom line.

So get out there and prepare to start shattering expectations.

## Notes

1.  theguardian.com, Dec. 15, 2013
2.  www.pcmag.com/article2/0,2817,2366104,00.asp
3.  http://newsfeed.time.com/2012/07/23/almost-everyone-doesnt-trust-the-internet/
4.  http://blogs.gartner.com/andrew_white/2012/04/16/do-we-trust-the-internet-too-much/
5.  http://fleishmanhillard.com/reputation-management/
6.  www.reputationinstitute.com/frames/press/CRO%20White%20Paper_%20RI%20UK.pdf
7.  Ibid.
8.  www.reputationinstitute.com/frames/press/CRO%20White%20Paper_%20RI%20UK.pdf

# Index

# About the Author

**Bill Walker's** professional background over 30 years combines reporting experience for Canada's largest newspaper with providing senior communications counsel to both public and private sector organizations.

For more than two decades at *The Toronto Star,* Mr. Walker worked in a variety of postings, including bureau chief at the Ontario Legislature at Queen's Park, parliamentary bureau chief in Ottawa, and Washington bureau chief during President George W. Bush's first term and the attacks of 9/11.

As a communications professional for the past decade, Mr. Walker has specialized in working with C-level executives and in leading teams to coordinate communications strategies for large corporations and government agencies and departments. He has worked extensively as a specialist in crisis communications, with an established track record working with complex, contentious issues. He works with partners through his company www.midtownpr.com.

He has conducted training for private sector CEOs, government ministers, heads of non-profits, and sports personalities. A frequent public speaker, he also appears on television and radio programs as a media commentator.